THE FORMS OF
VIOLENCE

Leo Bersani
and Ulysse Dutoit

THE FORMS OF
VIOLENCE

Narrative
in
Assyrian Art
and
Modern
Culture

SCHOCKEN BOOKS / NEW YORK

First published by Schocken Books 1985
10 9 8 7 6 5 4 3 2 1   85 86 87 88
Copyright © 1985 by Leo Bersani and Ulysse Dutoit

Library of Congress Cataloging in Publication Data

Bersani, Leo.
The forms of violence.
Bibliography: p.
Includes index.
1. Sculpture, Assyro-Babylonian — Themes, motives. 2. Sculpture, Ancient — Iraq — Themes, motives. 3. Violence in art. 4. Psychoanalysis and art.
I. Dutoit, Ulysse, 1944-   II. Title.
NB80.B4   1985   732'.5   84-22200

Designed by Cynthia Basil
Manufactured in the United States of America
ISBN 0-8052-3973-1

Acknowledgment is made for the permission to reprint the illustrations:

The Assyrian art reproduced in this volume is reproduced by permission of The British Museum.

Figure 1, scene from Leni Riefenstahl's *Triumph of the Will* (1935). Reproduced by permission of Films, Inc., Hollywood, CA.

Figure 21, *Still Life* by Giorgio Morandi (1953–54). Reprinted by permission of the St. Louis Art Museum. Gift of Prof. and Mrs. Theo Heimann, Tucson, AZ.

Figure 22, *Margaretha de Geer* by Rembrandt (1675). The National Gallery of London. Reproduced by courtesy of the Trustees, The National Gallery, London.

Figure 28, scene from Alain Resnais' *Night and Fog* (1955). Reproduced by permission of Films, Inc., Hollywood, CA.

Foreword

Late Assyrian sculpture carries a heavy burden in this book. It is the focal point of an esthetic and psychoanalytic argument about the imagination of violence in Western thought and art. We will be proposing that the anti-violent tradition of Western humanism has defined violence in ways which may actually have promoted an unintended fascination with violence. Our primary concern will be with that tradition's tendency to narrativize human experience as one of its principal strategies for making sense of experience. And we will offer, as an alternative to what we believe to be a complicity beween narrativity and violence, an approach to both history and art which emphasizes disruptive but nondestructive modes of understanding, perception, and desire. Can a relatively unfamiliar, ancient, Eastern, "peripheral" art carry the weight of this argument?

In one sense, it obviously cannot, and we confess from the start to having been seduced by something improbable, even "unacceptable," in our enterprise. We might insist, it is true, on the generally unrecognized greatness of the neo-Assyrian palace reliefs. We have ourselves been so dazzled by this art that we really should have no scruples about proclaiming that it deserves to be placed at the very summit of humanity's esthetic achievements. But what interests us in Assyrian sculpture is precisely something which discourages such statements. The lesson of disruptive mobility which we will find in these extraordinary works from the final centuries of Mesopotamian history includes a warning against those very orders of esthetic importance which might help us to justify our own undertaking. The appropriateness of our example is, perversely but unavoidably, inseparable from its fragility; in part, it suits our argument because it may *not* have the weight to carry it.

We will constantly be drawn to examples from the palace reliefs, but we will also constantly be moving away from the reliefs. A scene from the Lion Hunt in Ashurbanipal's North Palace at Nineveh will lead us to a text by Freud on the genealogy of sadomasochism; marching scenes from Leni

Foreword

Riefenstahl's *Triumph of the Will* will be placed alongside rows of kneeling Elamite subjects greeting their king Ummanigash on his arrival at Madaktu; and, in our argument about narrativity in art, we will be referring to the art historian E. H. Gombrich, to the realistic novel, and to Balanchine's ballets. Furthermore, our fifty-odd photographs are not intended as stabilizing illustrations of our text. Not only do they fail to give a comprehensive view of the palace reliefs; they also frequently ignore the principles of narrative framing so scrupulously respected in most of the previous photographic surveys of Assyrian sculpture.* We will at times be juxtaposing bits and pieces from narratively unrelated scenes. And in order to demonstrate the multiple or continuously displaced readings encouraged even by scenes in which the narrative emphases seem most rigidly defined, we have also photographed certain sections of the reliefs more than once, each time from a different angle of vision. Our photographs are interpretive and not merely supportive documents, and we recognize that our textual analyses are readings of images which are in themselves already analytic (visual) readings of the reliefs. That is, the photographs in this book record a certain adventure in visual attention, an adventure which we seek to replicate verbally in our written text. Not only does this express our skepticism about the possibility of *any* preinterpretive account of the reliefs; it also exposes us to certain errors, to what might be called mistaken replications in our readings of our own interpretive vision. The verbal text and the photographic text are juxtaposed readings of Assyrian art, and we include a few photographs unaccompanied by any specific commentary at all — photographs which the reader may find helpful in his or her resistance to our argument, a resistance initiated and invited by the mobility of our own text.

In short, a certain procedural restlessness in our work should make it impossible to settle on a single body of evidence or even a single version of our argument. One might speak of a digressive procedure, were it not for the difficulty of locating the "main line" of our development. Are the psychoanalytic essays a digression from an analysis of Assyrian sculpture, or does the latter interfere with a long Freudian speculation and break it up into three separate essays? Freud is crucial to our work: he has helped

---

*For some interesting exceptions to the general rule, see Amleto Lorenzini's photographs in R. D. Barnett's *Assyrian Sculpture in the British Museum* (Toronto, 1975), as well as in *Gli Assiri: La Scultura del regno di Ashurnasirpal II al regno di Ashurbanipal (883–663 A.C.)* (Foro Romano Curia: Istituto per L'Oriente, Centro per le Antichità et la storia dell'Arte del Vicino Oriente, 1980).

us to elaborate a theory of mimetic and nonmimetic desire which may account for conflicting psychic impulses to narrativize and to denarrativize our perceptions of reality. And yet even here, in the working out of three rather complex aspects of pyschoanalytic theory, our model has been the most speculative side of Freud, the side that is most mobile in terms of theory.

We are all familiar with dogmatic Freudianism. Especially in America, a kind of rigid Freudian orthodoxy has enjoyed an extraordinary prosperity, in terms of both medical (and therefore economic) and intellectual power. Freud's most authoritarian performances as a thinker have almost attained folkloric status in American culture. Recent developments in French psychoanalytic theory, however, have brought to our attention another Freud, one whose theory is insecure, incomplete, paradoxical, and even contradictory. This "other" Freud is difficult, but the difficulty has less to do with arcane conceptualizing than with a disarming and troubling tendency to discard doctrinal orders, to try out (and to move on *from*) various theoretical positions. The psychoanalytic essays in this book should be read as analytic fictions, as arguments which we have tried to pursue as rigorously as possible but which are themselves part of the elusive and disruptive psychic reality which they "describe." We are interested in writing which maintains a tension between rigor and extravagance; or, more exactly, in which logical orders run the risk of being exploded by virtue of their tendency to duplicate the moves of what they purport to describe. The fictive status of psychoanalytic theories does not mean that they "fail to meet" scientific criteria of truth. The very notion of such a meeting indicates a failure to recognize that theories of human desire repress their subject (both desire and the theorist) to the extent that they claim to be free of those disclosures or excesses through which desire enters discourse. Freud's theories of desire perform a certain violence against the very order on which their exposition depends. And perhaps the only guarantees we have of their "authenticity" are the agitations, and doctrinal uncertainties and mobility by which they are irremediably exposed as passionate fictions.

Much of what we say about dislocations and mobility in Assyrian sculpture could be used to describe modern art. The most original works of the last hundred years or so have accustomed us to fragmentation, continuously displaced emphases, and destabilized orders in art. But to discuss this disruptiveness as a uniquely modern phenomenon is to promote the myth of modern art as a "crisis," as a response to massive cultural dislocations which have, perhaps permanently, and tragically, unsettled the moral and esthetic orders of Western humanism. From this perspective, even the most sympathetic response to modern painting or literature is indistinguishable from a sense of loss: modern men and women have been cut off, alienated from possibilities of cultural harmony and wholeness. We wish to take the opposite point of view: the properties associated with modern art are not the property of any one historical period, and, while their reappearance may of course correspond to conditions of cultural crisis, they invite us to exploit the moves of consciousness — the perceptual and affective mobility — from which certain immobilizing cultural orders have alienated us.

To discover a similar invitation in the official state art of ancient Assyria has been especially gratifying to us. It is to be hoped that the very remoteness and unfamiliarity of the palace reliefs will prevent the reader from glamorizing — and dismissing — the displacements and dislocations in which they abound as the signs of a great historical crisis. Modern art has suffered from such dismissive glamorizing; what we would call a narrative sequestering of modernism in much modern criticism has given to the art of our time a dubiously privileged, nearly apocalyptic status in the "story" of our culture. By having our argument "lean" on some sculpture from ancient Assyria, we have chosen an art sufficiently marginal in that story so as to safeguard its disruptive power from the domesticating effects of historical interpretation. Indeed, our slender, distant prop looks more and more appealing as it seems less and less worthy of making weighty statements to the modern consciousness. At most, and at best, Assyrian sculpture will merely *move* us — not to define its "significance," but rather to experiment with meaning itself as an exercise in interpretive restlessness.

The palace reliefs photographed in this book are all part of the Assyrian collection of the British Museum in London. The caption identifying each figure designates the palace in which the scene was originally to be found and identifies the general section of relief slabs (as described in the British Museum catalog) from which each of our examples has been taken. These general identifications, as the reader will see, frequently do not describe the aspect of the action we have photographed; they are intended to specify the larger section of reliefs from which the illustration has been taken.

THE FORMS OF
VIOLENCE

Assyrian Palace Reliefs and Their Critics

From the ninth century B.C. through the reign of the last great Assyrian king, Ashurbanipal (668–627), the palaces of Nimrud and Nineveh were decorated with wall reliefs depicting scenes from Assyrian history. Most of the surviving examples of this art are now on view at the British Museum in London; the greatest number, and the most artistically impressive, come from the reigns of Ashurnasirpal II (883–859) and of Ashurbanipal. The palace reliefs are pictorial narratives in which Assyrian history becomes primarily a spectacle of extraordinary power. The celebratory nature of the reliefs, the obvious relish with which the defeat, humiliation, and slaughter of Assyria's enemies are portrayed, and the profusely gory detail of the battle and the hunting scenes, would seem to confirm the historians' view of the Assyrians as an intensely nationalistic, imperialistic, and violent people.

A modern analogue to the Assyrians' self-glorification in their art is Leni Riefenstahl's *Triumph of the Will*, the film which Hitler commissioned as a record and celebration of the 1934 Nazi Party Congress in Nürnberg. In the totalitarian nationalism of both Nazi Germany and ancient Assyria, the leader embodies the state. The visual means by which Riefenstahl realizes her apotheosis of the Führer are interestingly similar to those used by the Assyrian sculptors in their worshipful portrayal of Ashurnasirpal or Ashurbanipal. Riefenstahl's camera moves between an undifferentiated block of marching men (or the stereotyped variety of adulatory faces in the civilian crowds at Nürnberg) and the figure of Hitler, set off from all those surrounding him. In Mesopotamia, the king is portrayed twice as large as the surrounding figures, and the Assyrian sculptors, like Riefenstahl, even appear to use the principle of anonymous human alignments as a visual contrast

---

Figure 1: Scene from Leni Riefenstahl's *Triumph of the Will* (1935). **Figure 2:** The Elamite King Ummanigash is greeted on his arrival at Madaktu. *From the South West Palace at Nineveh.*

3

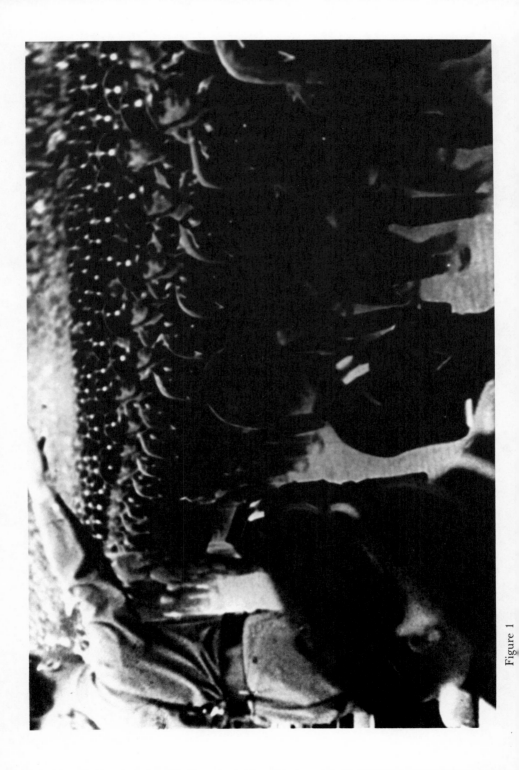

Figure 1

to the isolated, individualized king. Figure 2, for example, is part of a series which gives several versions of the same incident: superimposed rows of Elamite subjects on their knees or lying on the ground, frequently with their arms extended toward their leader, are paying homage to the upright figure of King Ummanigash on his arrival at Madaktu. Lining up human figures centers the one figure not in the line. The king, or the Führer, represents — he stands for and presents once again — his own columns of subjects; he *is* their national identity.

If we consider the Assyrian palace reliefs from the point of view of a narrative progression, the climactic moment or goal of all the apparently disordered, agitated battle scenes is an image of perfect immobility. The ceremonial alignments of victors and captives is the visual expression of the stable, unchanging *presence* of Assyria everywhere. Esthetically, the resolution of conflict is best shown by these sculpted tableaux which can be rapidly read; an almost dizzying line-up of similar figures spares us the trouble of having to guess, improvise, and try out possible modes of relation among different forms. The occupation of our visual field by identical forms is the esthetic order which celebrates a secure political hegemony.

Not surprisingly, Assyrian palace reliefs come off rather poorly in almost all discussions of ancient art. R. C. Barnett points out that the "lack of restraint and the exclusively one-sided obsession with the king's glory" distinguishes Oriental art from classical Greek art.[1] The example of Greece — more exactly, the example of fifth-century Greek art — has provided the normative model for the appreciation and judgment of art in Western culture. Seen against this model, Mesopotamian art in general — and the Assyrian palace reliefs in particular — lack "measure" and a "proper" distribution of emphases. Obsession with the king's glory in Assyria frequently takes the form of complacent illustrations of the king's brutality. H. W. F. Saggs speaks disapprovingly of the relish evident in pictorial accounts of Ashurnasirpal's brutal treatment of his conquered foes.[2] Art memorializes and glorifies the notorious atrocities of the Assyrians, who flayed, impaled, and burned prisoners. Eva Strommengen writes that for the Assyrians, only the propagandistic theme counts. One confirmation of this would be the fact that Ashurnasirpal's "standard inscription" (the broad bands of cuneiform text which separated the upper and lower bands of relief) is written right across the reliefs from his reign regardless of its esthetic irrelevance to the scene portrayed.[3]

The Assyrians' esthetic crudeness is, it would seem, the inevitable corollary of their inhumanity. Their taste for violence is of a piece with their inability to portray real human beings in a convincing manner. Consequently, Assyrian art, according to the eminent French scholar André Parrot, never moves us. It presents us with lifeless stereotypes; it lacks the expressive variety necessary to produce a powerful emotional response in the spectator.[4] As Strommengen writes, human relations are absent from this art as they are from all Western Asian art, in which human figures are like dolls with identical, masklike faces.[5] Parrot laments the fact that we have so few glimpses of daily life behind all the military scenes of Assyrian palace sculpture. It is with obvious relief that these writers refer to what they take to be the moments of naturalistic representation in this art: for example, the veristic narrative details in the work from Sennacherib's reign (704–681) and, more generally, the tendency beginning with Tiglath-pileser III (744–727) to make the reliefs more factual and less mythic, to transform them into credible historical narratives.

A. Leo Oppenheim has made the interesting observation that writing in Mesopotamia was used to freeze a tradition, not to adjust it to reality.[6] A slightly transposed version of this remark could be used to summarize the usual reservations about the Assyrian palace reliefs. The trouble with these reliefs would be, in effect, an almost fatal failure of adjustment. A preconceived, stereotypic notion of reality (and especially of human figures) precludes any accurate observation of reality. Given the history of Mesopotamian art, there is something mysterious about this. In third-millennium Sumerian art, as Parrot has pointed out, individuals stand out sharply; much later, it is impossible to distinguish Sargon from Sennacherib, or Ashurnasirpal from Ashurbanipal. Thus Malraux rightly warns that, contrary to what the history of Western art has taught us to expect, ". . . the evolution of Sumero-Akkadian art is not to be confused with a mastery of appearances," with successful imitation of the real world.[7]

The purposes of Assyrian art are narrowly political, its subjects are extreme forms of human violence (war and hunting animals), and it has only the most limited resources for representing the human figure. What possible point of contact can there be between a modern spectator and the pictorial account of the complacent brutalities of ancient kings? Essentially, Assyrian palace reliefs are condemned for what we will call narrative reasons. A certain idea—or, more precisely, a certain ideal—of narrative is superimposed on the reliefs, which are then judged to be deficient in the light of that ideal. The story they tell is not ours. Subjects of only peripheral human interest transmit a message of repellent violence.

Playing with Narrative

Could it, however, be possible that this very violence is a corollary of the narrative skills in which the Assyrians are presumed to be deficient? What the critics tend to condemn as an inadequate mastery of the art of narrative is, we would suggest, a kind of reduction of narrative to its essential principles — a reduction which reveals the congeniality of those principles to a violence which a variety of expressive narrative detail, for example, might have helped to disguise. In fact, the Assyrians move away from the violence attributed to them to the extent that they very artfully subvert (rather than cultivate) the techniques of narrative development. The question to be asked is therefore not "how good" the Assyrians are at narrative, but rather to what extent their sculpture is reducible to purely narrative accounts — accounts which, we believe inevitably stress the murderous violence of Assyrian history.

In the section from the Lion Hunt reproduced in Figure 3, we are irresistibly drawn to the point of maximal violence. The movements of the wounded lion on the left and of the two horses compel a rapid reading of the scene from left to right. Our eyes stop at what appears to be the dramatic center of the relief: the plunging of the horseman's spear into the lion's open mouth. But this anecdotal climax is ambiguous. First of all, the movement to the right continues *beyond* the climactic point. As a result, this movement does not merely serve the moment of violent contact between the animal and the man's spear; indeed, it carries the viewer away from that contact and thereby detracts from the impact of the lion leaping toward the left. If one looks more closely at this part of the scene (in Figure 4), it becomes even clearer that the juxtaposition of the two animals' opposite movements demand a continuously mobile reading of the scene rather than a visual stop at the lion's gaping, wounded mouth. Even an immobilized perception of the scene includes the tension of momentarily arrested movements. There are, furthermore, formal relations which distract the viewer from the violent subject. Note the parallelism of the several elements just below the spear

8

(a series comprising the rein, the harness, the lion's leg, and the horse's leg), as well as a similarity in the broken lines which constitute the outlines of both the lion's paw and the hunter's tassle just beneath it. Such formalizations could be thought of as repressing differences crucial to a narrative reading of the scene, and as thereby encouraging us to emphasize what might be called counternarrative organizations and identifications. The spear's iconological identity, for example, is rendered somewhat indeterminate by its participation in the triangle which it creates along with the rein below it and the part of the horse's mane between spear and rein. (Note also that the spear is raised out of its register to cut across the base line of the register above it.) One's interest moves between the geometric and the anecdotal at the very point at which the anecdotal center of the scene is being most strongly emphasized.

The force of this violent subject is, then, contravened by visual abstractions which disrupt the spectator's reading of the subject. It is true that relations could be detected among the formal elements of any representation at all. And we should say at the very outset of our analyses that we do not mean to suggest that Assyrian artists are unique in their subversion of visual story and their emphasis on formal play. Their work is, however, a particularly striking case of: (1) a highly narrativized art (in which the story line is frequently presented both in images and in an accompanying cuneiform text); (2) extraordinarily ingenious strategies for diverting our attention from the stories thus emphasized; and (3) a successful narrativizing of critical response. This last point is worth stressing, for while denarrativizing techniques could surely be discovered in almost all painting and sculpture, the criticism of art in our culture has predominantly responded to the narrative elements in art. This has been especially obvious, as we indicated a few pages back, in evaluations of the Assyrian palace reliefs; and we shall have occasion to see that even an art historian as sophisticated as E. H. Gombrich tends to identify the highest esthetic achievements with a mastery of narrative techniques. Western art, compared, say, to Islamic art, has had

---

Figures 3 and 4: Hunting wild onagers and slaying lions. *From the North Palace of Ashurbanipal at Nineveh.* **Figure 5:** Ashurbanipal in his chariot hunting lions. *From the North Palace of Ashurbanipal at Nineveh.* **Figure 6:** Ashurbanipal and the Assyrian army fighting the army of Teumman, King of Elam, at the battle of Til-Tuba on the River Ulai in 653 B.C. *From the South West Palace at Nineveh.*

Figure 3

Figure 4

Figure 5

Figure 6

an exceptionally strong narrative bias; but perhaps even more significant, culturally, is the way in which narrativity in art has so massively influenced our descriptive and evaluative vocabularies.

Certain manifestations of Western art have of course provided more support than others for this pervasive narrativizing tendency in our culture. The inclination to see stories in art, and, more profoundly, to use art as a kind of display of organizing principles serviceable for the narrativizing of human experience in general, is more effectively reinforced, for example, by Roman sculpture and eighteenth-century genre painting than by most modern art. The Assyrian palace reliefs are particularly instructive about a kind of sliding between narrative and nonnarrative modes of organization in perception and thought. Their appeal as the focal point of the argument we will be making lies less in the esthetic moves which subvert narrativity (moves discernible in most art) than in the paradigmatic clarity with which the reliefs trace an escape from the very type of response which they appear so powerfully to solicit. They demand, so it would seem, to be read narratively, but a narrative reading has led many critics to dismiss or at least to devalue them *for narrative reasons.* And this is perhaps inevitable unless, at the very moment we allow ourselves to be carried along by narrative interests, we find ourselves engaged in perceptual moves which undo narrative organizations and prohibit a fascination with the violent stories of Assyrian history.

The close-up of the Lion Hunt given in Figure 4 is a good introduction to the various kinds of formal play through which the Assyrians deemphasize their subjects. Because of this formal play, the mobility of the viewer's response is only partially determined by the violent movements which constitute the subject of the scene. Furthermore, our perceptual wandering from one part of a scene to another can also be experienced as a momentary epistemological uncertainty about the identities of certain forms (a leg or merely one of several parallel lines, part of a spear or one side of a triangle).

The element of play is especially evident in the palace reliefs depicting the Assyrians' military campaigns. Play in these scenes is largely a question of a profusion of forms. So many things are going on at once — as, for example, in Figures 7 and 8 — that we hardly know where to look. The intelligibility of Figure 7 is architectural rather than narrative. The chaos of human forms is contained within the spaces created by a few single lines: the curved line of the mountain toward the left and the two parallel horizontals toward the right. The latter two lines add to the number of incidents which may be represented (since wholly different scenes can logically be placed on either side of each line of demarcation), at the same time that they provide an ordering frame for the bewildering mass of actions. But in spite of such structuring elements, there is no one way to read the multiple activities of these large battle scenes. In Figure 9, we have a deceptive centering of all the action in the space between the top rungs of the two converging ladders. The ladders, as well as the men climbing them and the bowsmen to the right, all point to this apparently central space, but we are subtly moved into an entirely different direction by the curved line of prisoners descending toward the left on the bottom slab. And yet, as Figure 10 clearly shows, the horizontal line which begins about two-thirds of the way up the curve draws us away from the prisoners and toward the group advancing from the right. Because the horizontal line of the pole being carried by the first man in that procession is an extension of the right leg of the second man from the top of the descending curve, to look at the curve is already to begin looking away from it, to start moving toward the right.

Nothing is more typical of Assyrian art than such mobilizing strategies. Any focused point almost invariably includes the cues which keep us on the move. The sculptor manages simultaneously to bring a coherent centering to his scene and to transform every center into the margin of another (provisional) focus of our attention. Moreover, the connections from one section to another make it difficult to settle on one "right" reading of these scenes — a reading which might guarantee our visual progress toward climactic spaces. While there would of course be nothing unusual in the portrayal of movements coming from various directions in a battle scene, the reliefs devoted to the battle of the River Ulai suggest an exceptional indifference to what might have been thought of as the esthetically necessary holding power of the centering elements in a scene. We read not only from left to right on each slab; our taking in of the reliefs is always a complex sequence of horizon-

---

Figures 7 and 8: Ashurbanipal and the Assyrian army fighting the army of Teumman, King of Elam, at the battle of Til-Tuba on the River Ulai in 653 B.C. *From the South West Palace at Nineveh.* **Figures 9 and 10:** Capture of Ethiopians from an Egyptian city (probably a scene from the war of 667 B.C.). *From the North Palace of Ashurbanipal at Nineveh.*

Figure 7

Figure 8

Figure 9

Figure 10

tal *and* vertical eye movements, of movements from left to right and from right to left, of following a "story line" sometimes curved and sometimes straight.

As a striking example of the Assyrians' interest — an interest at once intense and yet also "light" — in physical violence, let's briefly consider one of their many images of men falling through the air to their death. The most interesting thing about the falling body in the upper central portion of Figure 11 is the number of forms created by its tangential contacts with the shield to the left, with the warrior climbing the ladder, and with the upper border of this section. Unlike superimposed forms, tangential forms create new shapes without changing the forms participating in these new shapes. In Figure 11, an extremely diversified group of new spaces is produced by the falling body's contacts with other surfaces. Thus the flying warrior prevents us from passively watching him "move." He mobilizes our attention by distracting us from his own tragic mobility, or by redefining it almost as a joyous occasion. It is not a question of denying the slaughter depicted in these images of battle. Rather, a playful puzzle of forms in the sculptural representation of this slaughter offers the spectator an alternative mode of agitation; the scene is calculated not to produce "esthetic calm," but rather to make us enjoy a kind of esthetic "violence": the agitations of multiple contacts producing multiple forms. The relation between the falling man and the Assyrian warrior climbing the ladder is not only one of a defeated victim to a brutal conqueror. They come together here in other ways: first of all, to produce the shapes enclosed by the lines of their adjacent bodies, and secondly, as a pleasant opposition of a movement upward and a movement downward. A certain beauty in both falling and climbing is brought out by the juxtaposition of these opposite movements. Each of the two figures reinforces, by contrast, the presence of the other, at the same time that the power of each is to refer to the other and thus to forestall the possibility, in the spectator, of a passive fascination with either figure.

Figures 11 and 12: King Ashurnasirpal directs the assault of a city by breaching, tunneling, and battering, while vultures hover overhead. *From the Throne Room in the North West Palace at Nimrud.* **Figure 13:** Capture of Ethiopians from an Egyptian city (probably a scene from the war of 667 B.C.). (Detail of Figure 9.) *From the North Palace of Ashurbanipal at Nineveh.*

Figure 11

Figure 13

Human Mastery over Nature

Perhaps nowhere in the history of art could we find such powerful images of physical agony as in the hunting scenes from Ashurbanipal's North Palace at Nineveh. The agony is of course that of animals and not of humans, and yet the details shown in Figures 14, 15, 16, and 17 seem to us especially good examples of a suffering so extreme that even the (animal or human) body's maximum resistance to it already resembles the body's abandonment to it. The sequence of Figures 17, 18, and 19 allows us to examine the agony of an Assyrian lion from varying distances. In 19, both the archer and the entire chariot's movement to the left work against any stabilizing of our attention on the attack to the right. Indeed, the only stabilizing factor at all in the scene is the large centered wheel at the bottom, the closed form of which contrasts with the energetic thrusting outward of the four figures in the chariot. But if we eliminate some of these distractions from our field of vision and concentrate on the attack to the right (in Figure 18), we are struck by a contrast within the act of violence itself. Expressiveness in these hunting scenes is always on the side of the animal victims; the hunters appear to be unaffected by their own violence. Not only do these hunters show no signs of excitement; more strangely (given the details with which the lions' physical agitation is skillfully represented), even the positions of the hunters' bodies seem unaffected by the weight of the massive animals lunging toward them.

Does this dramatic and peculiar contrast merely refer us to a ritualistic intention in the portrayal of this royal sport? It is frequently Ashurbanipal himself who is shown slaying a lion, and his very impassiveness could of course be thought of as part of a pictorial code by which the sculptors reverently refer to the king's — as well as to his hunters' — invincible power.[8] And

---

Figures 14, 15, 16, 17, 18, and 19: Ashurbanipal in his chariot hunting and shooting lions. *From the North Palace of Ashurbanipal at Nineveh.*

24

Figure 14

Figure 15

Figure 16

Figure 17

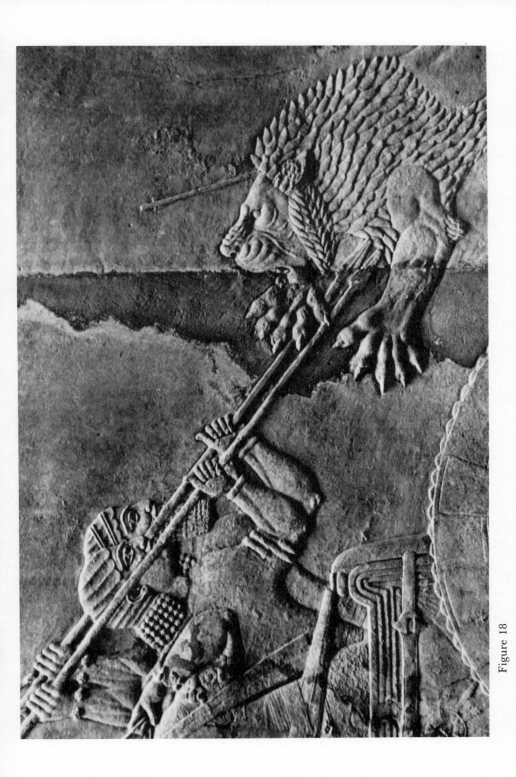

Figure 18

Figure 10

yet the social determinations of the hunters' calmly masterful pose (the pre-eminence of the royal party, the artist's flattering intentions) do not seem to us to exhaust its significance. For such social determinations are themselves perhaps always grounded in certain fantasies about the possibilities of human power in the world, fantasies contingently manifested by any presumably omnipotent monarch. Thus the possible tribute to the king (and, by a kind of metonymic contagion, to the entire royal hunting party) in the hunters' expressionless violence, far from being merely informative about signs of royal prestige and power in ancient Assyria, is also a stark manifestation of an unqualified human mastery over nature.

We wish to approach the problematics of this mastery through what may at first appear to be an inappropriate detour. We will juxtapose the Assyrians' hunting scenes with a modern speculative text on the relation between violence and affectivity among humans. In his 1915 essay "Instincts and Their Vicissitudes," Freud uses sadism and masochism in order to illustrate transformations in the objects and aims of instincts. He begins with a three-step process. The first step, which is somewhat confusingly called "sadism," is "the exercise of violence or power upon some other person as object." In step two, both the object and the aim change: the impulse to master is turned upon the self and its aim also changes from active to passive. Finally, the instinct returns to an object in the world, but since its aim has become passive, another person "has to take over the role of the subject," that is, the dominant role of step one. This last case, Freud points out, is what is usually called masochism. But he then goes on to make distinctions which profoundly modify the entire scheme just proposed:

> Our view of sadism is further prejudiced by the circumstance that this instinct, side by side with its general aim (or perhaps, rather, within it), seems to strive towards the accomplishment of a quite special aim — not only to humiliate and master, but, in addition, to inflict pains. Psycho-analysis would appear to show that the infliction of pain plays no part among the original purposive actions of the instinct. A sadistic child takes no account of whether or not he inflicts pains, nor does he intend to do so. But when once the transformation into masochism has taken place, the pains are very well fitted to provide a passive masochistic aim; for we have every reason to believe that sensations of pain, like other unpleasurable sensations, trench upon sexual excitation and produce a pleasurable condition, for the sake of which the subject will even willingly experience the unpleasure of pain. When once feeling pains has become a masochistic aim, the sadistic aim of *causing* pains can arise also, retrogressively; for while these pains are being inflicted on other people, they

31

are enjoyed masochistically by the subject through his identification of himself with the suffering object. In both cases, of course, it is not the pain itself which is enjoyed, but the accompanying sexual excitation — so that this can be done especially conveniently from the sadistic position. The enjoyment of pain would thus be an aim which was originally masochistic, but which can only become an instinctual aim in someone who was originally sadistic.[9]

Freud begins by discussing a *nonsexual* process in which masochism is derived from sadism. But by the end of the passage just quoted, sadism has become secondary, a masochistic identification with the suffering object. We would seem, then, to have two quite different kinds of sadism existing simultaneously once the infliction of pain has become an instinctual aim: an "original," nonsexual sadism which seeks to master the world, and a derived, sexual sadism which is actually a pleasurable fantasy-identification with the intense (sexualized) pain of the victim.

In his later work — and especially after the elaboration of his theory of the death instinct — Freud became even more emphatic about the priority of masochism. In "The Economic Problem in Masochism" (1924), for instance, he speaks of the libidinal life instincts attempting to make the death instincts harmless; they do this by directing our impulse to destroy toward objects in the external world, and this impulse "is then called the destructive instinct, the instinct for mastery, or the will to power" (SE, 19:163). Thus step one in "Instincts and Their Vicissitudes" turns out to be, like the sexual sadism which is really a projected masochism, a derived sadism. The implications of this shift (the beginnings of which are dramatically visible in the doctrinal uncertainty of "Instincts and Their Vicissitudes") are crucial for the nature of sexuality itself in psychoanalytic thought. In the passage quoted a moment ago, Freud moves toward the notion of specifically sexual masochism and sadism by suggesting that sexual pleasure may be a component of all sensations which go beyond a certain threshold of intensity. We find the same idea in *Three Essays on the Theory of Sexuality,* where Freud writes: "it may well be that nothing of considerable importance can occur in the organism without contributing some component to the excitation of the sexual instinct" (SE, 7:205). Pleasure and pain are therefore both experienced as *sexual* pleasure when they are strong enough to shatter a certain stability or equilibrium of the self. In passages such as these, Freud somewhat tentatively argues that the pleasurable excitement of sexuality occurs when the body's normal range of sensation is exceeded and when the organization of the self is momentarily disturbed by sensations somehow "beyond" those compatible with psychic organization. Sexuality would be that which is intolerable to the structured self.

The conclusion to which all this points is that sexual excitement is a function of masochistic agitation. In an analysis of our passage from "Instincts and Their Vicissitudes," Jean Laplanche emphasizes that "sexual pleasure [in Freud's scheme] resides in the suffering position."[10] He explains this by the nature of fantasizing, apparently assuming (correctly, we feel) that what Freud calls the sadist's "identification of himself with the suffering object" is conceivable only as a mental representation of that suffering. In fantasy, an object of desire is introjected; the pleasant or the unpleasant effect which the individual wishes to have on that object is therefore felt *by* the desiring subject himself. Human desire is restless not only when the object of satisfaction is absent; it is restless also because it perhaps always includes, within itself, the disruptive effect on the *other's* equilibrium which is now an effect on an internalized other. This seems to us the gist of Laplanche's argument, and the conclusion we would draw from this argument is that sexuality should be understood in terms of the reflexive pleasures of desire; *desire produces sexuality.*

Sexuality would be desire satisfied *as* a disruption or destabilization of the self. It would therefore not be originally an exchange of intensities between individuals, but rather a condition of broken negotiations with the world. The movement to satisfy a need (the "sadistic aim of inflicting pain," for example) becomes a desiring fantasy in which the structured self is more or less gravely "shaken" by an exceptional convergence between need and satisfaction. Perhaps the "threshold of intensity" which Freud speaks of is passed whenever this kind of *dédoublement* takes place. The excess intrinsic to sexuality would have to do with the excessive expenditure involved whenever the imagined effect of our appetites on the world is internalized.

We realize that these suggestions involve an extraordinary generalizing *and* limiting of sexuality. Laplanche is attempting to account for the very constitution of sexuality, and his reading of Freud leads him to displace the entire notion of sexual pleasure. Sexuality would no longer describe a particular type of encounter; rather, it would be definable in terms of the quantity of excitement (Freud) generated by the introjection of objects in desiring fantasy (Laplanche).[11] If, as Laplanche writes, "fantasy *is in itself* a sexual perturbation [*ébranlement*]," it is "intimately related, in its origin, to the emergence of the masochistic sexual drive." The activity of fantasy which constitutes sexuality in human beings is inherently an experience of "psychic pain."[12] And if we understand fantasy here as the imaginary expression and fulfillment of a desire, then the psychic disturbance produced by fantasy is an experience of pleasure *as* pain; that is, it is a masochistic sexual excitement. Sexuality — at least in the mode in which it is constituted — might even be thought of as a tautology for masochism.

Finally, it may be the masochistic excitement inherent in desiring fantasy which constitutes a destructive "instinct" — the Freudian death instinct — in the human subject. The death instinct can be thought of as accounting for a single process having two apparently distinct steps: the masochistic pleasure of desiring fantasy, and the ultimate or climactic masochistic pleasure of the end of desire. The nondesiring stillness of death is the sexual climax of masochistic fantasy. In one sense, masochism serves life. The threat to psychic wholeness in each destabilizing fantasy is an enrichment of being: masochistic excitement helps to destroy the structures and centers which lock the individual within a few repeatable patterns. But the logical "end" of such excitement — its goal and its termination — is the destruction of life itself. The Freudian death instinct simultaneously posits an enormously productive, psychically decentering sexuality and a sexuality identical with its own explosive and definitive end.

In its violent projects toward the world, the self would therefore also be shattered by the fantasized pleasure of its own annihilation. If sadism should always be understood as a derived and projected masochism, then the wish to arrest the movements of others would include the pleasure of restless desire finally being totally evacuated. Step one of "Instincts and Their Vicissitudes" posits a dissociation of sadomasochistic pleasure from sadomasochistic fulfillment. It refers us to the masochistic impulse wholly discharged, wholly dissipated, to a self no longer destructive but destroyed. The profoundly exciting nature of the ultimate exceeding of quantitative limits in the absolute "discharge" of death is, then, most adequately represented in an image which no longer contains any traces at all of excitement. Freud's nonsexual sadism is desire's interpretation of its life-serving affinities with death as nothing more than — death.

If we now return to Figure 18, we may be tempted to conclude that it represents the type of violence described in step one of Freud's scheme of sadomasochism in "Instincts and Their Vicissitudes." The hunt could be understood as carrying out a project to master part of the natural world; the strongest, potentially most violent beasts are subdued by the hunters' skillful power. And the latter exercise violence with no trace of excitement; as Freud says of "original" sadism, it does not aim at the production of pleasure through the infliction of pain. Furthermore, the coolness with which the lions are slain in the palace reliefs is consonant with a certain "estheticism" of which the sculptors themselves might be accused. A kind of relaxed virtuosity in the Assyrian images of leonine agony is at odds with the esthetic disruptiveness which we find most interesting in their work. We might even speak here of an uncharacteristic prettification of violence, a view of the hunt *only* from the perspective of its being an esthetically pleasing ritual. Figure 20, for example, gives us an anthology of poses. It is as if the subject of the hunt provided the artists of ancient Assyria with an exciting opportunity to experiment with unusual and dramatic formal arrangements. To a certain extent, they have a purely plastic interest in all these slaughtered animals. The sculptor can indulge in an extravagant play and tension of lines, shapes, and directions without transgressing the limits of realistic representation. As a result, we may feel that each lion stands out against an empty background, that it is isolated from the others in order that a formal tour de force may be better put on display. In this way, what we would call an immobilizing interest in forms is encouraged in the spectator. Each figure in this section of the Lion Hunt, it might be argued, has a self-contained expressive intensity, so that our attention is riveted and not mobilized by whichever part of the pictorial field we look at. Each lion is a perfect "esthetic" object; and the real subject of these violent scenes may even be thought of as the technique by which all violence has been denied.

The hunters' impassiveness lends some support to this way of reading the scene. The spearsmen attack their prey with a curious "esthetic" attentiveness. It is as if the viewer's proper response had been incorporated into the relief: both the hunters and the spectator are peacefully absorbed in a spectacle. In the case of the hunters, this instant of quiet attention is — somewhat incongruously, from a realistic point of view — also the moment of greatest violence: in Figures 5 and 18 for example (see pp. 12 and 29), the impassive hunters are shown plunging their spears into the lion's throat. They are less interesting to look at than the lion, but they appear to have the important function of telling us *how* to look at the lion. And it does not seem farfetched to say that the lesson is one of affectless violence — of that "nonsexual sadism" described in "Instincts and Their Vicissitudes" which, we have suggested, expresses a fantasy of self-displacing and self-shattering desire having been at last totally evacuated. The undisturbed human mastery of the doomed lion's energy gives us the image of an ideal, impossible control over the self and the world.

But an undiverted attention to isolated parts of a scene is, as we have

Figure 20

already had occasion to see, the exception rather than the rule in our responses to the Assyrian palace reliefs. Furthermore, even if we limit our attention to Figure 18, another reading is possible. For the hunters' impassiveness can be seen as evidence (and as a warning) that desire in the Assyrian palace reliefs will never be portrayed as a phenomenon of psychic projection. The reliefs solicit a type of passionate responsiveness to the world distinct from the mimetic or identificatory responsiveness which accounts for all the psychic movements described by Freud in "Instincts and Their Vicissitudes."

The question we are considering is this: how will the violence of the palace reliefs move us? As we saw a moment ago, one answer is to deny the validity of the question: we can forestall the agitations of violence by admiring violence as a finished esthetic product. And this controlled appreciation might be thought of as an esthetic derivative or by-product of the aim — described by Freud in step one of the quoted passage from "Instincts and Their Vicissitudes" — of mastering the world by immobilizing our response to it. Another possibility in the face of any spectacle of pain is, as Freud suggests, a sadomasochistic enjoyment of that pain. There is an ontological risk in this enjoyment, for it disturbs the centeredness of the self. It is as if we were somewhere "between" ourselves and the suffering victim, somehow ex-centric to ourselves in our identification with the victim's position (with the victim's pain). Finally, we may be moved merely to keep moving. The hunters' blankness may be the cue for a nonmimetic response on the viewer's part. That is, the hunters' way of considering the lion helps to block movements of identification with violent scenes; instead of moving toward the content of such scenes in a kind of mimetic fascination, we may simply move away toward other representations. The hunters' expressive blankness would therefore frustrate our imitative impulse.

It is this last possibility which will interest us most in this discussion. It will provide the basis for esthetic and moral speculations at odds with the dominant esthetic *and* ethic of mimesis in our culture. The process described in "Instincts and Their Vicissitudes" is one of imitative self-displacement. Freud suggests that the pleasure of sadism is inconceivable except as a

---

Figure 20: Ashurbanipal in his chariot hunting and shooting lions. (This scene is continuous with — to the right of — the scene represented in Figures 18 and 19; a detail of it is shown in Figure 15.) *From the North Palace of Ashurbanipal at Nineveh.*

phenomenon of "sympathetic" projection. The only psychologically intelligible explanation of the sadist's enjoyment of the suffering of others is this: that he is, precisely, enjoying that suffering. He has introjected the self projected into the suffering position of the other. But the fantasy-identifications outlined by Freud may be crucial to *all* sympathetic responses to suffering.[13] We generally take the value of such projections for granted. They are assumed to be central both to our responses to art and to our capacity for moral behavior. But our reflection on Laplanche's reading of Freud leads us to suggest that "sympathy" always includes a trace of sexual pleasure, and that this pleasure is, inescapably, masochistic. If this is the case, there is a certain risk in all sympathetic projections: the pleasure which accompanies them promotes a secret attachment to scenes of suffering or violence. We are not, it should be stated, arguing (absurdly) "against" sympathy. Rather, we wish to suggest that the psychic mechanism which allows for what would rightly be called humane or morally liberal responses to scenes of suffering or violence is, intrinsically, somewhat dysfunctional. The very operation of sympathy partially undermines the moral solidarity which we like to think of as its primary effect. Our views of the human capacity for empathetic representations of the world should therefore take into account the possibility that a mimetic relation to violence necessarily includes a sexually induced fascination with violence.

The works of the Marquis de Sade point to the same conclusion. Indeed, Freud might have found in Sade an explicit argument for the connection between mimetic sexuality and sadomasochistic sexuality. In Sade, sexual excitement is a shared commotion. Sade suggests that we do not have sex with others *because* they excite us; excitement is the consequence of sex rather than its motive. And this is because it is essentially a replay in the libertine of the agitation he produces on the other's body. In the funny physiological terms in which Sade sums up the Duke's ideas in *The 120 Days of Sodom:* "He noticed that a violent commotion inflicted upon any kind of an adversary is answered by a vibrant thrill in our own nervous system; the effect of this vibration, arousing the animal spirits which flow within these nerves' concavities, obliges them to exert pressure on the erector nerves and to produce in accordance with this perturbation what is termed a lubricious sensation."[14] The libertine's pleasure depends on the transmission of his victim's "commotion" to his own nerves; his own "vibration" *is* that commotion.

Physical violence is the necessary consequence of this view of sexuality in Sade. If erotic stimulation depends on the perceived or fantasized commotion of others, it becomes reasonable to put others into a state of maximal commotion. The libertine's erection-provoking vibrations increase in direct proportion to the visible intensification of his victim's suffering. In a profoundly ironic way, Sade's sadism is consistent with the theories of benevolent sympathy which he scornfully rejects. For what he rejects is not the mechanism of sympathetic projection assumed by theories of benevolence, but rather the pious view that we are stirred by *virtuous* identifications with others. Virtue is irrelevant to the agitation induced by the suffering of others. It is the identification itself — that is, a fantasmatic introjection of the other — which appears to be intrinsically sexual. Such introjections make us "vibrate"; they destroy psychic inertia and shatter psychic equilibrium. Interestingly enough, both Sade and Laplanche use the word *ébranlement* to describe this psychic shattering which produces what Sade calls *une sensation lubrique* and which for Laplanche characterizes our inescapably fantasmatic sexuality.

A mimetic relation to violence may itself be promoted by certain modes of representing violence; indeed, we are about to consider the possible affinities between narrative organizations of experience and the mimetic impulse. But Assyrian sculpture has already suggested to us other representational strategies, and these strategies appear designed to stimulate a nonprojective, nonimitative participation in suffering or violence. By devaluing the content of any one scene of violence, the Assyrian sculptors train us to formalize psychic mobility. It is of course true that narrative content itself must be conveyed by formal means, and we will now be speaking of those formal principles most congenial to narrative designs. For the moment — and without denying that the distinction proposed here is to a certain extent a heuristic one — we would argue that mobility becomes a response to formal stimuli in the Assyrian reliefs, stimuli which forestall movements of identification with the narrative content of any representation. Thus, even in Figure 18, where our attention would seem to be unavoidably focused on a subject of violence, the very mode in which our attention is directed to that subject moves us away from it and toward those lines and forms which, as we saw in Figure 19, mobilize our attention when we are looking at the larger scene. In the Assyrian palace reliefs, the very centers of anecdotal violence decenter themselves.

Narrativity and Violence

Narration is exciting. In *The 120 Days of Sodom,* the account of the libertines' activities is organized according to the principles which govern the reminiscences of the four female narrators. As a result of this dependency of the Sadean narrative on other narratives within it, Sade's work is exceptionally instructive about the affinities between violence and the ways in which we organize experience in order to make sense of it. The carefully constructed stories of Mme. Duclos and her colleagues have an aphrodisiac effect on the libertines. But storytelling is valued because it is *already* a certain type of erotic activity. Like much erotic literature, *The 120 Days of Sodom* moves from comparatively mild sexual anecdotes to orgies of erotic violence. But Sade points out that this is not the order in which his characters have the experiences being related. We are told that on a particular day, for example, Sade's heroes were engaged in activities which will be *narrated* only as part of the record of a later day. In other words, the progress from one day to the next in Sade's book is not determined by "real" chronology (by the lived experience of the characters designated as real people by this fiction); rather, the work is organized in order to produce a certain type of narrative progression which is itself erotically stimulating. The purpose of the book is, we might say, to create its own narrative.

But this is not a "merely" formal strategy; it is the means by which the reader is brought to share the characters' feasts of sex and violence. While Sade's narrative doesn't reproduce the "actual" simultaneity of fellatio, flagellation, and coprophagia, it does reproduce the pacing which is more deeply characteristic of Sadean sex than the sexual content of any one day's adventures. That pacing could be characterized as a calculated movement toward explosive climaxes. And the movement is made possible by the isolation and imprisonment of the object of desire: the Sadean master removes his victims from the world, or a particular desire "removes" a part of a body from the rest of the body. The master's authority and self-possession in Sade depend on the *limited relations* available both to his own desiring fantasies and to the "detached" object of desire as a result of such removals. In other terms,

40

the calculation, preparation, and control of climaxes result from the establishment of foregrounds (objects of desire) and backgrounds (insignificant, undesired reality). This is also a narrative strategy: the climactic significances of narrative are made possible by a rigidly hierarchical organization of people and events into major and minor roles. In narrative, coherent orders are the privilege of a world in which relations have been limited to precisely those from which a central coherence can be made to appear "naturally" to emerge. Finally, however, we might also note that the calculated progress of a Sadean narrative is toward a violent act which, in a sense, puts an end to all calculation. The ideal climax in Sade is murder. The Sadean story works toward definitive and not merely provisional closures, which are in themselves both the logical *dénouement* of a narrative line and a radical repudiation of all narrative lines whatsoever.

Sade is, of course, an extreme example, but his work is less of an anomaly in our culture than a kind of scandalous paradigm of our preferred strategies for eroticizing the accounts we produce of our experience. At another level of interest, E. H. Gombrich curiously corroborates Sade's confidence in the affective powers of narrative. In *Art and Illusion,* Gombrich speaks of the "constant interaction" in the history of Western art "between narrative intent and pictorial realism." It was the discovery of "the character of Greek narration" — narration "concerned not only with the 'what' but also with the 'how' of mythical events" which revolutionized classical art in antiquity. We are moved by Greek art because of a narrative genius which stirs our "imaginative sympathy" for the events and characters of that art. Thus the cultural audience which Gombrich has in mind, like Mme. Duclos' listeners, are excited out of themselves and into new identities as a result of high narrative skills. Such skills are also a sign of esthetic realism for Gombrich: the accuracy of art's imitations of reality would seem to be intimately linked to narrative modes of imitation.[15]

Actually, the question is more complicated than Gombrich suggests. As Roland Barthes, among others, has argued, the relations between realistic description and narrative can appear to be oppositional. Barthes has singled out certain passages in Flaubert and Michelet as literary examples of a certain descriptive excess over the manifest needs of the narrative. He speaks of the "useless details" in such passages, details which, instead of serving the purpose of narrative intelligibility, announce the independence of "the real" (or *le vécu, le vivant*) from any structural function at all. In a similar vein, Michael Fried has, with great originality, drawn attention to what he calls scenes of absorption in painting. Such scenes function in the Western tradition, according to Fried, as characteristic matrices for realistic representation, and in them the pictorial narrative, while not annulled, is, significantly, suspended.[16]

It could, however, be argued that what Barthes calls "the great mythic opposition" between *le vécu* and the intelligible is a superficial one even within the art which appears to sustain it. On the one hand, as Barthes suggests himself, if the narrative intelligibility of the classical *récit* depends on a distinction between "the probable" or *le vraisemblable* (the law of Poetry) and "the real" (the law of History), the probable is itself a type of imitation, and in a sense it is more realistic (more universally true) than the isolated "real" detail. On the other hand, with modern realism, Barthes writes, a new notion of the probable is born which can be identified as the "referential illusion." The signifier now is meant to refer directly to the real, and the signified (*le signifié*) is expelled from the verbal sign. That is, *both* the narrative intelligibility of the *récit and* the narratively "useless" detail certify the work of art's realistic intent. The details in modern realism serve the narratives which they temporarily suspend; they provide narrative schemes with just that dose of the superfluous and of the inert, which qualifies and therefore renders more acceptable (more realistic . . .) the potentially mechanical order and potentially excessive intelligibility of narrative development. The "useless details" evoked by Barthes *belong to* (rather than transgress) narrativity. In this respect, nothing is more instructive than the failed attempts by Alain Robbe-Grillet (a writer heavily promoted by Barthes) to let those *effets de réel,* those pure object-signifiers, stand by themselves, detached from story, from classical narrative progressions. All his critics — including, eventually, Barthes himself — provided the superficially absent narrative lines for *The Voyeur* and *Jealousy;* the "neutral" or "designifying" *récit* turned out to be simply a (not overly subtle) psychological puzzle, structured (behind the apparent disorder) with the prototypical narrative rigor of a detective story. And, once restored to narrative intelligibility, his books began to look very much like more or less conventional realistic fiction. In short, however "artificial" we may occasionally recognize narrative organizations to be, it is as if we have most easily recognized reality in narrative representations of reality. The dominant mimetic strategy in our culture has been a narrative one. Gombrich rightly connects our sympathetic projection into the work of art with the narrative tendency in art. What he does not do is to question the nature and value of this projection, the implications of its dependence on narrative, and our reasons for finding narrative art realistic.

These are precisely the issues which we wish to investigate. The palace reliefs suggest a curious ambivalence toward narrative: the Assyrians simultaneously celebrate themselves through story and divert our attention away from the story line of their sculpture. The question of perspective in the visual arts is important here. Assyrian sculptors seem to have had little sense of perspective. They make use of what has been called vertical perspective: background scenes are simply placed above foreground scenes. Furthermore, the disproportionate size of a human figure on an Assyrian palace relief expresses that figure's political or religious importance rather than his physical place in the scene and his distance from the observer. But this technical naïveté serves an acutely energetic perception of reality. The discovery of perspective in Western art helped to make main subjects stand out and to encourage the illusion that these subjects are unrelated to the spaces surrounding them. What is the value of this illusion in art? The rendering of depth on a flat surface has none of the practical value of the perception of depth in the physical world. In the latter, we obviously need some reliable sense of how far objects are from us, which ones are placed in front of or behind or to the side of others, and what their distances are from one another. The reproduction of the third dimension in art is at once an impressive and a useless achievement. Our negotiations with the represented objects in painting and sculpture in no way resemble our dealings with real objects. In painting, we inertly contemplate an artificial version of that picture of space which is the condition for our action in the world. Our fascination with effects of depth in art is perhaps a fascination with those properties of our own vision which allow us to manipulate reality outside of art.

The denial (or ignorance) of the dimension of depth in art can work as a corrective of certain perceptual habits which are necessary outside of art. Some of the most interesting Western painting since the discovery of perspective has included what may seem like a perverse indifference to the presumed advantages of that discovery. It has not been a question of returning to the obvious awkwardness of most preperspectival painting. Rather, in painters as different as Rembrandt, Monet, Cézanne, and Morandi, we have what might be called an effort to return the background to the areas of significant form in art. In a Morandi still life, for example, the space surrounding a group of vases becomes as formally significant as the vases themselves. And in Rembrandt's later work — the self-portraits, as well, for example, as the paintings of Jacob Trip and Margaretha de Geer in the National Gallery in London — there is practically no distinction between the human body and "mere" background. The achievement of these paintings is not, it seems to us, in some realistic rendering of the discolorations, the asperi-

Figure 21

Figure 21: *Still Life* by Giorgio Morandi (1953–54) St. Louis Art Museum. **Figure 22:** *Margaretha de Geer* by Rembrandt (1675). National Gallery of London.

44

Figure 22

ties, and the cracking of aging skin surfaces. Much more interestingly, Rembrandt uses the effects of age on the body as an occasion for connecting the human to the nonhuman. He does not, however, *de*humanize his subjects, depriving them, from a tendentious psychological perspective, of some specific human dignity. There is nothing naked or exposed about these figures; they haven't been caught at the moment of some shocking physical or psychological truth. Instead, Rembrandt paints what might be called the egalitarian effects of matter. He gives us much more than the particular physicality of individual human subjects; his work suggests the equal physicality of all substances in the world. Consequently, Rembrandt's emphasis on the fact that his faces are, literally, made of paint, is not a self-conscious reminder that this is art. On the contrary: it suggests that, from the most realistic and referential point of view, the old woman's and the old painter's faces — beyond and before the work of art — are and always have been *materially related* to the paint used to portray them, and this essentially mysterious connectedness in the universe both deflates the pretensions of the human and exalts the *presence* of our world.

The subversion of perspective reminds us of presences which our practical operations in the world naturally lead us to neglect. The reinstatement of these presences is essentially an antinarrative enterprise. Perspective is intimately linked to narrative vision. The perception of objects diminishing in size within a visual field of variable distance is a structuring event analogous to the organizations of experience in narrative. The coherence of narrative depends on the establishment of priorities: stories move ahead only if a principal drama emerges and works toward a climax against a background of secondary or general characters and events. In the most general sense, we have narration whenever one thing is placed in front of something else which it partially blocks. In narration, we submit ourselves to hierarchical orders of recognition rather than to the mobility of a forgetful perception which dismisses centers and reconstructs temporary orders with each of its moves.

More interesting than the Assyrian sculptors' presumed ignorance of techniques for rendering depth is what we take to be their deliberate avoidance of effects of perspective. In the fragment of a battle scene represented in Figure 23, we immediately see, thanks to the clarity of the general narrative line, that the horizontal legs on the left in the upper section are in front of the tree and that the fallen soldier is behind two standing warriors. But if we look closely at the left part of the scene (Figure 24), we should also

46

notice certain spatial confusions. The tree is surely behind the legs, but the legs occupy no privileged foreground. The limbs appear to be a variation of the tree's form; the effect is one of juxtaposition rather than of superposition. (And we should emphasize that this is true of the relief itself, and is not merely the effect of a necessarily flattening photograph.) The similarity between the volumes of the man's toes and the volumes of the tree's leaves reinforces our sense of foot and tree as related forms rather than as subject and background. Thus, while we know what is going on where, we also see that things are going on from one form to another which have little to do with the anecdotal sense of the scene.

This undermining of narrative priorities is strikingly illustrated in Figure 25. In a sense, the hunter's hand is not *on* a lion's leg. It seems to us more accurate to say that we have a leg, then a hand, and then a claw, and that the juxtaposition of these different forms is the principal subject or even message of the image. The bulging muscles on the animal's leg may be realistically justified, but this very consideration allows the artist to defeat realistic positioning and to make the leg as high on the relief as the hand in front of it. Also, the hunter's hand is a flat and simple surface compared to the animal's claw and leg; thus, the element which would normally be in a privileged foreground position is put to a certain disadvantage by the luxuriant forms (the complex curved volumes) above and below it.

The subversion of the narrative subject, and of those techniques which help to make the subject stand out sharply against a more or less subordinate background, is crucial to the Assyrians' treatment of violence. In thus working against their own narrative accounts of the violence in Assyrian history, these ancient sculptors tend to problematize the very notion of violence, to make it difficult for us to think of violence as a subject unique in itself, a subject easily identifiable and easily isolated. We usually think of violence in terms of historically locatable events; that is, as a certain type of eruption against a background of generally nonviolent human experience. In this view, violence can be made intelligible through historical accounts of the circumstances in which it occurs. Such accounts, like almost all historical writing, are narrative in that they elaborate story lines as a way of mak-

---

Figures 23 and 24: Ashurbanipal and the Assyrian army fighting the army of Teumman, King of Elam, at the battle of Til-Tuba on the River Ulai in 653 B.C. *From the South West Palace at Nineveh.*

Figure 23

Figure 24

Figure 25

ing sense of experience. Violence is thus reduced to the level of a plot; it can be isolated, understood, perhaps mastered and eliminated. And, having been conditioned to think of violence within narrative frameworks, we expect this mastery to take place as a result of the pacifying power of such narrative conventions as beginnings, explanatory middles, and climactic endings. [17]

Obviously, the elaboration of a story line, with clearly established foregrounds and backgrounds, and proceeding according to the conventions just mentioned, does not exhaust the possibilities of narrative. Historically, narrative has been a much less well-defined, less homogeneous phenomenon than this general description suggests. We have been referring to a paradigm of narrativity frequently transgressed in the history of narrative. Literary narratives, for example, often do *not* progress, with linear causality, toward climactic *dénouements*. Everyone is familiar with narrative works (such as *The Arabian Nights* and many eighteenth-century European novels) in which what is presumably the main story is so habitually interrupted or postponed as to disappear almost entirely from the narrative foreground. The latter is taken over by a succession of secondary or digressive stories which can make the very category of principal story not merely problematic but even superfluous. What has been called the embedded narrative—in which story A includes story B which includes story C, and so on—defeats narrative progression by the very multiplication or, more exactly, by the recommencements of narrative interest. Finally, apocalyptic narratives (such as the *Book of Revelation*) accumulate climaxes in addition to developing toward them; to a certain extent, they deemphasize beginnings and middles and allow the entire narrative space to become a repetition of climactic moments. [18]

But, in most of these cases, the transgressive play is obvious. That is, a familiar, deeply ingrained habit of narrativity is being violated, and much of the interest in works which do not fit the simple paradigm we have outlined lies in their defiant reference to that paradigm, their self-conscious refusal to conform to it. The cultural importance of linear narrative as a pervasive mode of organizing and making sense of experience cannot be measured by the number of "pure" narratives which a culture produces. In the past twenty years or so, what almost amounts to an industry of narratology has invaded academic criticism. The results of all this narratological

Figure 25: Return from the hunt. *From the North Palace of Ashurbanipal at Nineveh.*

research have not been very enlivening; indeed, the number of people involved in such research may strike us as a more significant argument for the cultural centrality of narrative than anything that has been said *about* narrative. Nevertheless, these studies, by documenting the distance between narrative principles and narrative practice, have usefully emphasized — by a kind of negative proof — the importance of narrative models as conditions of possibility for narrative performance.

In one sense, the Assyrian palace reliefs are as close as any art we know to the simplest model of linear, nontransgressive storytelling. As we have seen in the examples already chosen, if we respond primarily to the narrative presentation of violent events in this art, we are led to isolate and to immobilize the violent act as the most significant moment in a pictorial plot development. And the narrative sequestering of violence produces the ideal conditions for a mimetic relation to violence. Our analysis of the Freudian genealogy of sadomasochism led us to conclude that such a relation to spectacles of violence includes a sexually induced fascination with it. The immobilization of a violent event invites a pleasurable identification with its enactment. A coherent narrative depends on stabilized images; stabilized images stimulate the mimetic impulse. Centrality, the privileged foreground, and the suspenseful expectation of climaxes all contribute, in historical and artistic narratives, to an immobilizing self-displacement; that is, to the type of identificatory representations outlined by Freud in "Instincts and Their Vicissitudes." The historian's or the artist's privileging of the subject of violence encourages a mimetic excitement focused on the very scene of violence. The atrophied relation of that scene to adjacent (but background) activities blocks our own relations to those activities and limits the mobility of our attention and interest.

The Assyrians appear to accumulate scenes of horror with a singular complacency — and this has been an important factor in the distaste one senses even in the admiration of Mesopotamian scholars for their art. But the violent *spectacle* never maintains a privileged position in the palace reliefs. The

---

Figure 26: Ashurbanipal and the Assyrian army fighting the army of Teumman, King of Elam, at the battle of Til-Tuba on the River Ulai in 653 B.C. *From the South West Palace at Nineveh.* **Figure 27:** King Ashurbanipal triumphs over the allies of Shamash-Shum-Ukin. *From the North Palace of Ashurbanipal at Nineveh.* **Figure 28:** Scene from Alain Resnais' *Night and Fog* (1955).

Figure 26

Figure 97

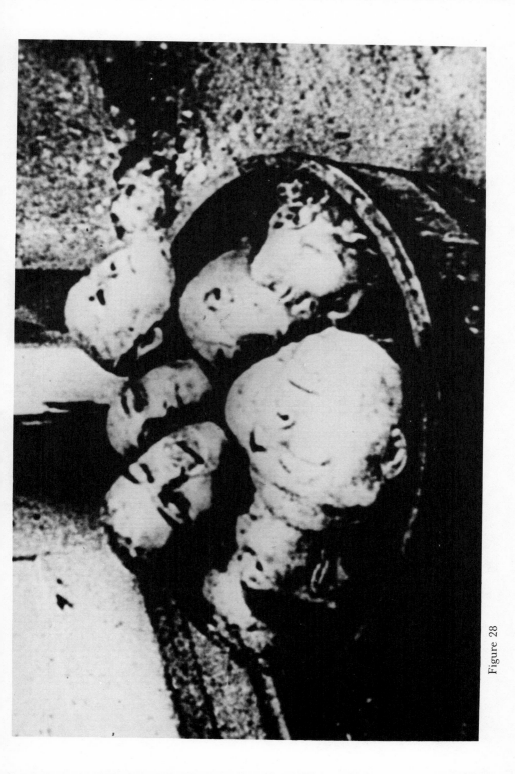

Figure 28

Assyrian sculptors' relation to their own narrative line is not exactly transgressive (and therefore deeply reverential). Rather, it is as if they strategically saturated themselves in linear narrativity as a way of escaping from it, of disrupting its orders. It is precisely in following a narrative movement toward centers and climaxes of violence that we move *away from* that movement (and those centers) to supplemental, nonnarrative points of interest. The Assyrians are intriguingly dismissive toward the very feats of violence which they celebrate. They never deny or disguise their talent for narrativizing violence. They take for granted our interest in that talent, at the same time that they prevent us from being arrested by what it produces. We might say that the assumption of this art is that we cannot help but be interested by narratives of violence, but that we are also always ready to follow marginal interests which disrupt narrative and which prevent the reading of violence from becoming a fascinated identification with acts of violence.

The palace reliefs are enormously suggestive not only about esthetic responses, but also about our moral relation to history. Or, more exactly, these scenes of war and of the slaughter of animals could be taken as a model of art proposing — and training us in — a way of resisting the seductive power of historical violence. The Assyrians refuse to melodramatize. The very casualness with which they treat violence is instructive. The brutalities of war and of hunting are somewhat trivialized in their artistic re-creations. The great scenes of Assyrian history always include cues which, in spite of the undoubtedly celebratory intentions of these ancient artists, invite us to dismiss the historical seriousness of such scenes, cues which displace our attention and thereby prevent the stable reading of static images. Assyrian sculpture adopts a subversive passivity in front of Assyrian history; it simultaneously celebrates and reformulates the "glory" of that history. As a potential corrective to our fascination with violence in history, Assyrian art does not propose a myth of nonviolence. Instead, in the course of allowing us (of forcing us) to see, even to enjoy, examples of the violence in which human history inescapably implicates us (Figure 28),[19] it also stimulates those psychic dislocations of mobile desire which may help to forestall a destructive fixation on, and complicity with, anecdotal violence.

56

Relations

Relations are everywhere. The Assyrians frequently suggest this through echoes or extensions from one section of sculpture to the section just below or above it. We have already commented on the top section of Figure 23 (see page 46); if we now consider both parts of that scene, we see that the two are connected. Note the series of roughly parallel horizontal lines which "connect" the fallen bodies in both slabs, as well as the diagonal line leading from the spear in the bottom scene to the leg just left of center in the upper scene. Figure 29 presents more complex relations between two vertically adjacent scenes. There are first of all oppositional relations: between the movement to the left at the top and the movement to the right in the lower scene, as well as between the upper rectangles and the lower circle. But there are also certain formalizations which slightly blur the differences in content between the two scenes in the interests of a counternarrative relatedness. Note, for example, the parallelism of the extended bottom bar of the lion's cage and the shaft in the scene below it. Also, parts of both scenes are included in a single structural frame by virtue of the fact that one could draw a straight vertical line from the left side of the man's cage to the middle of the wheel and the chariot carriage's left corner, as well as from the right bars on the man's cage to the point of contact between the chariot's right border and the wheel. Such relations suggest that the sculptor's eye, as he works on one part of the wall, "contains" images of an adjacent section, either as a mnemonic residue of work already done or as part of his peripheral vision. One scene is executed partly in function of the other; it becomes a kind of formal answer to it, through elements of contrast or of repetition.

These effects in Assyrian art remind us of the importance of chance relations in the universe. Mere juxtaposition creates formal relations, and in a sense the world is nothing but juxtaposed forms. The palace reliefs are of course highly artful products, but they also refer us to nonhuman designs (such as the patterns on mineral stones, or the changing designs of pebbles on a beach), as well as to unmotivated, unintended meetings and

57

Figure 29

contacts (such as the accidental similarities which craftsmen discover, after their work is done, among different sections of a patchwork quilt). Assyrian sculpture is full of such likenesses, and yet they never do away with difference or heterogeneity. There can even be something humorous in this inevitability of relations. For they are both unexpected and unilluminating; they point to nothing more solemn or significant than to a certain economy in the distribution of forms. It is because the fish are near the trees in Figure 30 that we notice a resemblance between their shapes and the shape of the branches, but that resemblance tells us nothing about the characteristics of either fish or leaves. It refers us to a joke in nature itself, the joke of a frequent bad fit between the repertory of forms and the repertory of identities. Such oddities can be illustrated in the most genial of spirits, for they testify simultaneously to a boundless diversity in nature as well as to a certain degree of reliable familiarity in any form we may encounter. Material traces or inscriptions are always finally repeated.

And yet there is never any question about the individual identities of similar forms in Assyrian sculpture. The fish in Figure 30 do not become the leaves whose form they partially share, nor do they become merely an oblong shape. Similarly, we can note casually, without speaking of identities as if they were abstractions, the resemblance between the lion's eye and the central part of the warrior's bracelet in Figure 31. This points to something very important in the Assyrian palace reliefs: the similarities we note among various forms do not function as a unifying force. Not only do formal likenesses suggest nothing about the "essence" of the related objects; more strangely, they do not even suggest that one form could be substituted for the other.

Nothing could be more alien to these entertaining, almost accidental similarities than the metaphoric reduction of difference to sameness which, in a famous passage of *Remembrance of Things Past*, the Proustian narrator

---

Figure 29: King Ashurbanipal fighting lions on foot and pouring a libation over dead lions. (Description of a three-register composition, of which only two registers are shown. Ashurbanipal shoots an arrow at the lion emerging from the cage in the left section of the upper register.) *From the North Palace of Ashurbanipal at Niveneh.* **Figure 30:** The Elamite King Ummanigash is greeted on his arrival at Madaktu. *From the South West Palace at Nineveh.* **Figure 31:** Ashurbanipal in his chariot hunting lions. (Detail of Figure 5.) *From the North Palace of Ashurbanipal at Nineveh.*

Figure 31

admires in Elstir's paintings. The passage is worth looking at briefly, for it is one of the most transparent examples in Western literature of the use of metaphor as an epistemological strategy for *unifying* phenomena. The "charm" which Marcel finds in each of the seascapes in Elstir's studio at Balbec consists "in a sort of metamorphosis of the things represented in it analogous to what in poetry we call metaphor; God the Father had created things by naming them, it was by taking away their names or giving them other names that Elstir created them anew." Elstir renders things "not as he knew them to be but according to the optical illusions of which our first sight of them is composed." Such illusions are, for Proust, equivalent to truth; we have them at "the rare moments in which we see nature as she is, with poetic vision." The pictorial metaphor which the narrator then describes consists in the suppression of all demarcations between the land and the sea:

> It was, for instance, for a metaphor of this sort — in a picture of the harbour of Carquethuit, a picture which he had finished a few days earlier and at which I now stood gazing my fill — that Elstir had prepared the mind of the spectator by employing, for the little town, only marine terms, and urban terms for the sea. Whether its houses concealed a part of the harbour, a dry dock, or perhaps the sea itself came cranking in among the land, as constantly happened on the Balbec coast, on the other side of the promontory on which the two were built the roofs were overtopped (as it had been by mill-chimneys or church steeples) by masts which had the effect of making the vessels to which they belonged appear town-bred, built on land, an impression which was strengthened by the sight of other boats, moored along the jetty but in such serried ranks that you could see men talking across from one deck to another without being able to distinguish the dividing line, the chink of water between them, so that this fishing fleet seemed less to belong to the water than, for instance, the churches of Criquebec which, in the far distance, surrounded by water on every side because you saw them without seeing the town, in a powdery haze of sunlight and crumbling waves, seemed to be emerging from the waters, blown in alabaster or in sea-foam, and, enclosed in the band of a particoloured rainbow, to form an unreal, a mystical picture.[20]

Proust elevates a kind of confused subjectivity to the status of an objective truth about the world. The goal of art would be to recapture the "errors" of our original vision (a vision uncontaminated by intelligence) — or, to take an example from another register of Proustian experience, to record the temporal errors of "involuntary memory," of those sudden invasions of the present by a past sensation, invasions which place us somewhere between past and present. In Proust, this "betweenness" occasionally seems to consist of a constant movement in the psychic space between the terms of all relations, but it can also be a detemporalizing essence. The major tension of his work is, precisely, between a view of relations as dislodging the self from all fixed positions and another view of relations as allowing us to disengage timeless qualities in which a self may be permanently fixed.

A much-quoted passage on metaphorical activity in *Time Recaptured* belongs to the latter position. "Truth" in art, the narrator writes,

> will begin only when the writer takes two different objects, establishes their relationship — analogous in the world of art to the [unique relationship established by the law of causality in the world of science] — and encloses them in the necessary rings of a beautiful style, or even when, like life itself, [comparing qualities shared by two sensations, he makes the essential nature common to both sensations stand out clearly] by joining them in a metaphor, in order to remove them from the contingencies of time . . .[21]*

Perceptual errors (errors of vision but also, as in Marcel's involuntary memories, of smell and of touch) provide a physiological model for the epistemological virtues of artistic style. The writer and the painter should deliberately cultivate those illusions which blur the distinctness of individual objects. For each such illusion may be the sign of a hidden quality common to different objects (or to different moments of time), a quality which can perhaps be made to appear without the objects (or outside of time). The demarcation between past and present, between land and sea, fade; juxtaposed objects are fused in a transcendental identity; and the heterogeneous space of human life would be replaced by a unifying, homogenous space of essences.

The great moments of metaphoric conjunction in Proust's novel correspond to the abolition of spatial and temporal intervals. The differential texture of the narrative itself is set against a kind of memorializing metaphoric tendency in the text which abstracts (and, in the form of universal laws, makes explicit) the qualities common to different types of experience (sexual passion and social snobbery, the moves of diplomacy and the tactics of a military campaign). In the Assyrian palace reliefs, on the other hand, visual analogies are subverted by the obstacles we encounter — the other forms — if we attempt to proceed directly from one term of the analogy to the other. This is by no means the case in all visual art: painters, for example, can

*Material in brackets is translated by the authors.

easily clear the field between two points in order to emphasize a relation and to establish a unifying visual theme. But the Assyrians create relations partly by directing us away from relations of resemblance. Consider the underwater scene in Figure 32. The circles of water are related not only to the eyes of the fish (by resemblance) but also to the rest of the water (by contiguity). They therefore cannot exist only as a metaphoric term; they are also part of a surface, and nothing encourages us to skip *any* surfaces even as we connect two separated circles. Indeed, to make the connection we pass through interesting space which diverts us from the connection. The eye and the circle thus also connect through spaces which do not resemble them at all. They *touch*, ultimately, through the mediation of other forms.

Figure 32: Ashurbanipal and the Assyrian army fighting the army of Teumman, King of Elam, at the battle of Til-Tuba on the River Ulai in 653 B.C. *From the South West Palace at Nineveh.*

Figure 32

Fetishisms and Storytelling

In psychoanalytic theory, the relation between metaphoric and metonymic substitutions is crucial to the problematics of desire. In *The Interpretation of Dreams,* Freud defines desire as a psychic movement which aims to revive perceptual memories associated with the satisfaction of a need (SE, 5:565–66). The revival of such perceptual memories would be a hallucinated repetition of a past satisfaction. The *movement toward* this exact repetition is desire. Both desire and hallucinated satisfaction are inseparable from images of satisfaction; or, to use the proper Freudian term here, they are both *activities of fantasy.* Before physically going toward an object of desire, we psychically go toward it (and, to a certain extent, already find pleasure in it). Fantasy is a relation of desire to an internalized absent object. The difference between hallucinatory fantasy and desiring fantasy is that while the former is experienced as the exact repetition of a remembered pleasure, the latter is by definition a sort of mistake, an *in*exact version of the pleasurable experience. Because of this, desire is always on the move: always somewhere "to the side of" the experience it presumably wants to revive, desire continuously changes one image for another and is thus intrinsically an unending process of displacements and substitutions.

In a sense, the objects of our desires are always substitutes for the objects of our desires. But in what sense, exactly? Should we assume that there *are* real objects of desire, or, more radically, that there is a privileged model or paradigm of desire from which all our desires derive and to which they always ultimately refer? Or, to put this last question in another way, is desire intrinsically fetishistic? In a short essay of 1927, Freud traces fetishism in men to the child's repudiation of the absence of a penis in women. If, as Freud claims, the child explains this absence as the result of the woman having been castrated (everyone "originally" had a penis), then his repudiating her lack of the male genital organ is a way of denying castration — and, most importantly, a manner of protecting himself from castration. In fetishism, this negation takes the form of an intense sexual interest in certain objects

66

or parts of the body — underclothing or feet, for example — which "take the place" of the missing phallic organ. Desire for these objects is, then, not really desire for the objects themselves, but rather for the presence of that object whose absence they both designate and deny.

To say that fetishism provides the model for all desire could mean that the objects we desire are always merely derivative substitutes of at least theoretically locatable and definable "primary" objects of desire. In this view, desire would attach itself to "wrong" objects not because this wrongness is a function of desire's productivity, but because there is a "right" object which makes the productivity itself essentially spurious. We wish to make a very different argument: the very notion of fetishism in Freud can be used against what could be called a fetishistic theory of desire (that is, a theory determined to *have* a founding object of desire, to repudiate its absence just as the fetishist repudiates the absence of a penis in women).

Almost half of Freud's very brief essay on fetishism is devoted to a discussion of "ego-splitting." He recalls having formulated, in an earlier work, "the proposition that the essential difference between neurosis and psychosis was that in the former the ego, in the service of reality, suppresses a piece of the id, whereas in a psychosis it lets itself be induced by the id to detach itself from a piece of reality." But not long after having written this, Freud analyzed two boys who had refused to acknowledge their father's death, "and yet neither of them had developed a psychosis." The mind can, apparently, split, part of it recognizing a real fact and part of it repudiating the same fact. "It was only one current in their mental life." Freud writes of his two young patients, "that had not recognized their father's death; there was another current which took full account of that fact. The attitude which fitted in with the wish and the attitude which fitted in with reality existed side by side." In the same way, fetishists have a "divided attitude . . . to the question of the castration of women." They do not psychotically deny that women lack a penis; consequently, they do not hallucinate a penis onto the woman's genitals. The beliefs of the child who will later become a fetishist are by no means unaffected by his perception of the woman's real body. He retains his belief that the woman has a penis, but he also gives it up. A "compromise" is reached according to the terms of which "the woman *has* got a penis, in spite of everything, but this penis is no longer the same as it was before. Something else has taken its place, has been appointed its substitute, as it were, and now inherits the interest which was formerly directed to its predecessor" (SE, 21:154, 155–56).

The exact relation between the penis and its "substitute" is not quite clear in the essay. Freud calls the fetish a substitute penis, but he also says that the organs or objects selected for this role generally do not act "as symbols for the penis in other connections as well." A fetish is not a phallic symbol; it does not necessarily resemble the penis. What is preserved as a fetish is very often "the last impression received before the uncanny and traumatic one." Feet and shoes, for example, were on the way up, in the child's line of vision, to the woman's genitals. Similarly, underclothing can "crystallize the moment of undressing, the last moment in which the woman could still be regarded as phallic" (SE, 21:155).

We find it significant that the view of the fetishistic object should *precede* the traumatic sight. It is as if nothing followed that sight. The child does not search afterwards in his repertory of images for something similar to the penis; he is indifferent to symbolically appropriate objects. Rather, it seems more important for him to return to a moment preceding the shock. The terrifying lack is too powerful to be denied, and therefore the child does not "return" the penis to its proper place. Instead, he simply repeats the experience *without quite having it*. The moment which initiated the trauma is treated as a terminal point never reached. The fetishist could therefore think of his aversion to the female genitalia as the result of his attention and desire having been arrested by something more interesting, more desirable, on the way to the woman's genitals.

Fetishism is an intriguing narrative jumble; it is fundamentally an antinarrative phenomenon in that its principal strategy is to confuse a certain story line, to deny both beginnings and climaxes. The trick is to transform the moment at the origin of the fetishistic object's powerful appeal (that is, the sight of the woman's genitals) into an event already too late for any such investment of affect. The fetishist can see the woman as she is, without a penis, because he loves her with a penis somewhere else. The crucial point — which makes the fetishistic object different from the phallic symbol — is that the success of the fetish depends on its being seen as authentically different from the missing penis. With a phallic symbol, we may not be consciously aware of what it stands for, but it attracts us because, consciously or unconsciously, we perceive it *as* the phallus. In fetishism, however, the refusal to see the fetish as a penis-substitute may not be simply an effect of repression. The fetishist has displaced the missing penis from the woman's genitals to, say, her underclothing, but we suggest that if he doesn't care about the underclothing resembling a penis it is because: (1) he knows that it is not a penis; (2) he doesn't want it to be only a penis; and (3) he also knows that *nothing* can replace the lack to which in fact he has resigned himself.

There can be something ridiculously inappropriate in the fetishist's choice of an object. He works, as it were, with whatever is at hand, with the nearest or most accessible thing. In fetishism, the irreducible difference between the adored object and the sexual organ which it has been chosen to replace means that fetishistic desire, for all its obsessive fixation on a single object, is inherently disoriented and confused. As a result, it may promote a mobility of the desiring imagination to which it at first seems logically and irremediably opposed. It is, in a sense, a model of desire detaching itself from one image and moving on to other images. Freud speaks of the fetishist's detachment from any interest in the woman's genitals, and of his displacing that interest onto another object. But this very denial of castration could be taken as a sublimated enactment of it. Desire is "cut off" from its object and travels to other objects. Thus the very terror of castration can initiate us into those psychic severances which guarantee the diversification of desire. The anguished denial of castration can have the paradoxical effect of deconstructing and mobilizing the self. For the resolute effort to satisfy the singleminded wish to possess a phallic mother helps to move the child away from the mother, to derange his *system of desiring* by the absurd, even laughable objects designed to replace the missing phallus.

Even more absurd is what might be called the ontological distance between the fetishistic object and the female genitalia. A phallic symbol replaces the perceived penis; it has attributes similar to those of a real phallus. But what the object in fetishism (a foot, underclothing) and the woman's genitals have in common is a fantasy-phallus, one that never existed in reality. In discussing fetishism, we have been using the verb *replace,* which is perhaps misleading. The fetish can't replace *or* re-place anything, since it signifies something which was never anywhere, neither in the woman's genital area nor in her clothing. Rather, the fetish is an inappropriate object precariously attached to a desiring fantasy, unsupported by any perceptual memory.

Fetishism is a singularly insubstantial sickness. One final piece of evidence can be adduced: the fetishist's ambivalent attitude toward his fetish. "To point out that he reveres his fetish," Freud writes, "is not the whole story; in many cases he treats it in a way which is obviously equivalent to a representation of castration." Thus the fetish can be treated with tenderness or hostility, and Freud sees these attitudes as corresponding to the denial and the recognition of castration. But why should the fetish be treated with hostility? Freud argues that treating the fetish in a way equivalent to castrating it "happens particularly if [the fetishist] has developed a strong identification with his father and plays the part of the latter; for it is to him that as a child he ascribed the woman's castration" (SE, 21:157). To develop all the implications of this remark would require a much longer discussion of Freudian theory. Let it suffice to say that the condition for "normal" heterosexual desire—the boy's identification of his desires with those of his father—would seem to include the desire to castrate the woman. Is it, then, possible for heterosexual desire (as it is defined in Freudian theory) ever to divest itself entirely of the fantasy of violence which was a fundamental act of interpretation in the child—his interpretation of how the woman lost her penis?

Freud claims that the fetish "saves the fetishist from becoming a homosexual, by endowing women with the characteristic which make them tolerable as sexual objects" (SE, 21:154). The fetishist, we might say, is in a no-man's-land: in the gender-land of neither the heterosexual nor the homosexual man. Both male heterosexuals and male homosexuals see the woman as having lost her penis. For male homosexuals, according to Freud, this loss makes desire impossible, while male heterosexuals, quite literally, fill in the gap in intercourse; they return the penis to its proper place. This concern with castration would, in the Freudian scheme, be just as strong in homosexual desire, with the difference that if the homosexual identifies more strongly with the castrated mother than with the castrating father, *his* repetition of the original, violent gender-differentiating act will involve his desiring the castrating, atoning father (who can return the homosexual's own penis to him at the same time that he deprives him of that dangerous organ which, making him resemble the father, also makes him a terrible threat to the woman). Homosexuality would thus be nothing more than an oblique, fearfully reserved version of male castration-fantasies.

In this scheme, the fetishist exhibits an interesting uncertainty. Does she have one, or doesn't she have one? Does the fetishist want to harm the woman's phallus or revere it? Is he restoring the phallus or taking it away? Is the object the phallus, or something else? The fetishist's desire is unique in that it lacks interpretative security. However jumbled the heterosexual and homosexual fantasy-scenarios outlined in the last paragraph may sound, they can all be coherently structured on the basis of a single firm conviction: the woman has lost her phallus. The fetishist, who is essentially neither heterosexual nor homosexual, enjoys no such conviction. He has looked away too quickly. Having both seen and not seen, he will insist that he saw what he didn't see and yet also insist that he saw what he in fact did see. And all this troubled seeing will go on elsewhere — with an irrelevant object perhaps there and perhaps not there, perhaps a phallus and perhaps a knee or a piece of fur. The profound undecidability of the fetishist's relation to his fetish is strikingly illustrated in the case Freud mentions of

> a man whose fetish was an athletic support-belt which could also be worn as bathing drawers. This piece of clothing covered up the genitals entirely and concealed the distinction between them. Analysis showed that it signified that women were castrated and that they were not castrated; and it also allowed of the hypothesis that men were castrated, for all these possibilities could equally well be concealed under the belt — the earliest rudiment of which in his childhood had been the fig-leaf on a statue (SE, 21:156–57).

Our discussion has been perverse: can the fetishist, a person often exclusively attached to a single object for the satisfaction of his sexual needs, really be used almost as a hero of uncertain desire, of undecidability? But in the sense which interests us we are not speaking of the actual man who must caress and, perhaps, stamp on a stocking or a piece of underclothing in order to arouse himself sexually. The fixation which makes him a fetishist is, we might say, his unfortunate, his erroneous reading of the original *movement* of his fetishism. For fetishism depends on an ambiguous negation of the real, a negation which mobilizes the desiring imagination. This negation creates an interval between the new object of desire and an unidentifiable first object, and as such it may be the model for all substitutive formations in which the first term of the equation is lost, or unlocatable, and in any case ultimately unimportant.

What we wish to propose, then, is that the process which may result in pathological fetishism can also have a permanent psychic validity of a formal nature. The individual may, as it were, return to the woman's genitals in heterosexual desire or even through the detours of homosexual desire, but he may also continue to profit from the fetishistic configuration of his early relation to the mother's body. This profit would consist of the general mobility of his desires and a more or less implicit recognition that the objects of desires are always fantasy-objects. What he wished to replace was never there, and the replacement never resembled the missing penis. No image of desiring fantasy ever reproduces the object (or image) which it may be designed to replace. What goes "wrong" in clinical fetishism is perhaps

71

an insufficient degree of castration. This phrase, for all its apparent absurdity, can nonetheless be used to describe an inability to detach oneself from the phallus itself. To be fetishistically attached to certain privileged objects is, in a sense, to deny castration more forcefully than it is denied by the fetishistic object itself. For such an attachment proclaims what the fetishist *has* to know is a lie: the equivalence between his adored object and the phallus. It is as if he *had* seen a phallus to which a substitute could be referred, by which it could be measured, whereas he is a fetishist precisely because he saw an absence which he partially accepts by going elsewhere to deny it.

The double bind of fetishism is avoidable only if it remains in the personality as a formal model of desire's mobility. Or, in the terms which we have been using to discuss Assyrian sculpture, the psychic movement in fetishism is one which establishes relations in contingent, even accidental, fashion. Connectedness can never be equivalence, and to find a term of comparison is already to know the need of moving on to other terms (related and yet incomparable). Freud's essay on fetishism is all the more interesting to us in that it describes a visual process. The drama of fetishism is a perceptual drama: it consists of a fundamental adventure in human seeing. Both the risks and the (provisionally saving) securities of vision are outlined in this theoretical treatment of symptoms apparently designed to abolish all risk from vision. Nothing is stranger than this secret dismissal of the phallus in Freud's explanation of the fetishist's nearly mad reduction of differences to a permanent phallic presence. And this very dismissal encourages us to recognize the uselessness of the phallus as a term of comparison (as *the* term of comparison). The shock of "castration" can thus have the beneficent result of detaching desire from the phallus, and of promoting the discovery of new surfaces.

Bows, Curves,
Marching, Dancing

Characteristically, the Assyrians tend to emphasize tensions and to initiate circuits of perceptual movement even in their treatment of those forms which lend themselves most easily to static effects. As we can see in Figures 33, 35, and 36, the many bows in the palace reliefs create frames which might isolate the enclosed elements of a scene from the elements of the scene outside the bow. The frame does have a centering effect (which seems especially strong in 33), at the same time that it subverts this effect by creating a space for formal relations irrelevant to the anecdotal unity of the larger scene. In 33, the archer and the man with the hatchet, to the extent that they share the space within the bow, are partially removed from their narrative functions and come into contact simply as juxtaposed surfaces. Furthermore, the arc-shaped enclosure is set against the strong horizontal lines of the arrow and the archer's arm, as well as against the dominant diagonals of the spears. As Figure 34 shows, the principal structural lines of this scene are the diagonal lines of three "V's." This structure brings us both toward and away from the central frame. The tree is emphatically outlined by parallel (or near-parallel) lines between it and the bow and the spears; the tree becomes almost as strong a formal presence as the central arc. Finally, as Figures 33 and 36 illustrate, the frame of the warrior's bow is frequently open. The man's body forms one of its sides, and the elliptical enclosure thereby opens out — through, for example, the long irregular line made by the archer's head and arm in 33 — toward other forms. Ambiguously cen-

---

Figure 33: Ashurbanipal and the Assyrian army fighting the army of Teumman, King of Elam, at the battle of Til-Tuba on the River Ulai in 653 B.C. *From the South West Palace at Nineveh.* **Figure 34:** Diagonal V-structure of Figure 33. **Figure 35:** Arming the king in his chariot. *From the North Palace of Ashurbanipal at Nineveh.* **Figure 36:** Ashurbanipal in his chariot shooting lions. (Detail of Figure 19.) *From the North Palace of Ashurbanipal at Nineveh.*

73

Figure 33

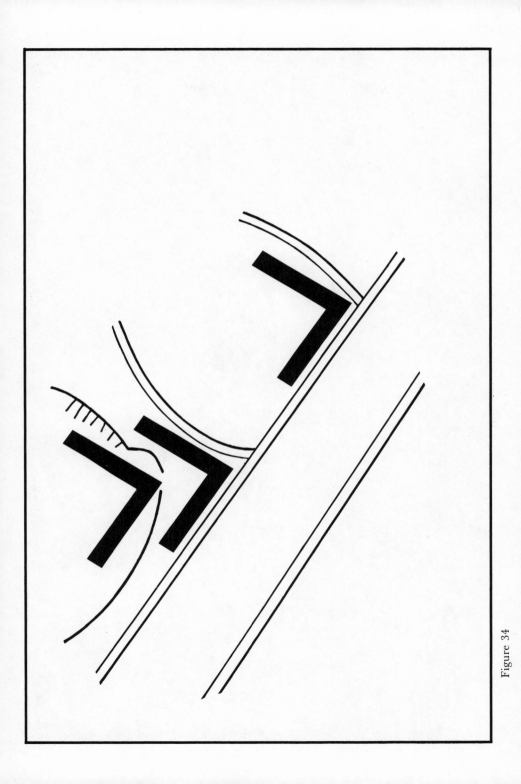

Figure 34

Figure 35

Figure 36

tered and imperfectly closed, Assyrian bows thus fail to immobilize our attention on pictures which frequently explode their frames.

Figure 37 is a remarkable example of the Assyrian sculptors' interest in complex formal play. The scene is executed almost as an exercise in plotting possible relations between curved and straight lines, at the same time that each element in the exercise has a strong narrative identity. Formal play in the palace reliefs never becomes another, more abstract system which would simply replace the sequential logic of narrative. While the Assyrians frequently use the reliefs as a workshop for testing various ways in which different forms can be related, their forms always constitute recognizable objects. In a sense, this renders an accurate description of our response to the reliefs virtually impossible. For our reading takes place, as it were, in the undefinable "space" between narrative representation and the play of repetition and difference among multiple forms.

This play is especially intricate in Figure 37. The shape of a bow exemplifies only one of the relations possible between a curved line and a straight line. In a bow, the curve interrupts the straight line's horizontal extension, while the latter breaks the circular movement of the arc. This type of relation is repeated in Figure 37 in the form just to the right of the bow, although now the arc is below rather than above the straight line. But the point of contact (or of near contact) changes if we turn the curve upside-down — which is exactly what the sculptor has done in shaping the line of the fallen warrior's right buttock just below the suspended bow. The curiously central position of the bow both subverts the anecdotal violence in the scene (the bow is given at least as much emphasis as the man's head) and provides the simplest formal model for much more complex oppositions between straight and curved lines. Especially rich relations can be traced between the bottom of the horse's body and the upper part of the man's body. For here the same element includes both curved and straight segments (see the warrior's leg, for example), and as a result the relations between the two bodies are at times relations between straight lines, at other times between two differently curved lines, and at still other points between a straight line and a curve. The bow surely owes much of its strange power in this scene to the contrast between the simplicity of *its* contrasting lines (although even

---

Figure 37: Assyrian chariots and cavalry charge enemy archers, with vultures hovering overhead. *From the Throne Room in the North West Palace at Nimrud.*

Figure 37

here we should note that the bowstring itself is not quite straight), and the complicated, shifting nature of the relation between the animal and human figures which frame the elongated space in which the bow is poised. Finally, a kind of formal transition between the bow and its frame is provided by the arrow that disappears into or behind the fallen man's buttocks.

The reliefs from the reigns of both Ashurnasirpal II and Ashurbanipal contain scenes of men and animals lying under the stretched bodies of moving horses or camels. Not only does this motif provide the Assyrian sculptors with opportunities to displace their emphasis from a violent anecdote to a play of relations between curved and straight lines; it also allows them to depict an astonishingly tender violence. In Figures 38 and 39, the defeated bodies are enveloped rather than trampled on by the racing animals above them. The brutality of these images of hunting and of war is qualified by a rather mild sensuality: the almost protective sensuality of long, sinuous bodies covering but not touching other bodies.

The study of straight and curved lines in the visual arts is instructive about some of the ways in which perception can be made to serve political purposes. A straight line could be considered as a perceptual model of exact repetition. In a sense, the eye's movement along the surface of a straight line is a pseudomovement. For the only perception we have of the change or the difference which is the sign of our having moved from one point to another is not in the line itself, but in its changing contexts. If we could see a straight line in empty (context-free) space, our eyeball's mobility would, as it were, never be confirmed by the perception of differences in our visual field. In these ideal conditions, a straight line would promote a visual mobility at once controlling and nonproductive. Nothing would divert us from our initial direction, and nothing would be produced by the movements we make. The situation is more ambiguous with curves. On the one hand, to follow the direction of even a simple curve is to exercise a visual mobility which registers differences within the field of vision. The eye movements themselves are more complex: a vertical curve, for example, is followed not only by vertical eye movements but also by movements of the eye to the right and to the left. An extended curve of some complexity is perhaps the simplest visual experience we can have of the world as a continuous, continuously diversified space, as a space too heterogeneous to be reduced to a single structural account of it. To follow the shifting directions of such a line is to submit to a visual mobility which produces differences and which we only partly control. The eye is not passive; it actively fails to dominate its field of vision.

This distinction is important, but it can easily be abolished. There are certain curves which produce difference only to reinforce the power of sameness. We are thinking especially of the curves traced by cradling movements back and forth between the same terminal points. To be cradled or to watch a cradling movement is to experience a continual repetition of the same differences. Cradling simultaneously gives us the pleasure of movement and the security of returning to those positions where we would still be had we not moved at all. Significantly, the arc produced by cradling hides multiple straight lines (see Figure 41). The cradling movement itself is a detour which, without traveling along these straight lines, does nothing but reach, over and over again, their terminal points as half circles on these virtual straight lines.

The curved line traced by a cradling movement has a more insidious appeal than a straight line. For while a perfectly straight line could be taken as a geometric metaphor for a deathlike world in which change (and therefore time as well as differentiated space) has been eliminated, the very fact that it leads us always in the same direction allows us not only to abbreviate our perception of it but also to become inattentive to it, to turn away from it. In cradling, we enjoy mobility within a rigorously controlled range of differences. Cradling seductively combines mobility and exact repetition; it gives us the illusion of difference within the reality of sameness. The certainty of always returning to the same points encourages the passivity peculiar to being cradled or to watching cradling movements. Nothing is more hypnotically tranquilizing than movement without surprises. Most appropriately, we put infants to sleep by rocking them gently; cradling—somewhat like breathing—is a minimal experience of the agitations intrinsic to life; it is an agitation compatible with the immobility of sleep.

In *Triumph of the Will,* Leni Riefenstahl expertly cradles us with her curving lines of marching soldiers. When the marchers break into a curve (as

---

Figure 38: King Ashurnasirpal hunting lions from his chariot. *From the North West Palace at Nimrud.* **Figure 39:** Assyrian chariots and cavalry charge enemy archers, with vultures hovering overhead. *From the Throne Room in the North West Palace at Nimrud.* **Figure 40:** Siege and captives of Hamanu in Elam. *From the North Palace of Ashurbanipal at Nineveh.* **Figure 41:** Virtual straight lines in arcs.

Figure 38

Figure 39

Figure 40

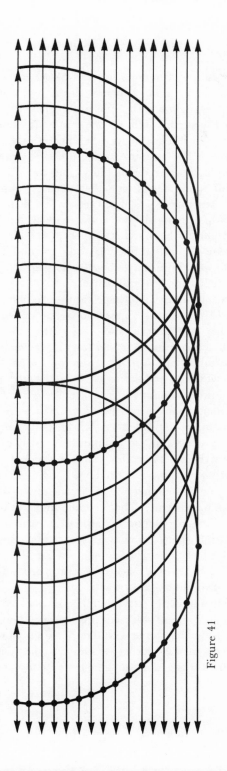

Figure 41

they turn, for example, from one street of Nürnberg into another), we are not freed of the monotonous sameness of the military march; rather, we are subjected to the hypnotic rhythms of sameness in motion. In the ranks of the perfectly executed march, no one draws attention to himself; the individual suppresses all movements different from the synchronized movements of the mass. The military parade presents the impressive spectacle of a radical simplification of the mobility characteristic of living organisms. And that simplification is the result of the marchers' submission to an *order* — a command and a structure — which succeeds in suggesting that the same body can occupy multiple points in space at the same instant. If a spectator's gaze were fixed on a part of the marchers' itinerary at which a new direction inflects the procession's straight line, he would see nothing but repetitions of that change and would thus have the curious spectacle of a perfect equivalence between repetition and difference.

Riefenstahl is not an immobile spectator of military processions in *Triumph of the Will*. Indeed, she appears to be fascinated by movement: the movements of her own camera, and those of the people and objects in the scenes which she films. But one of her favorite movements is the unfurling of flags (or the "unfurling" of flames from torches held in the air); that is, a movement in which an undulating curve is repeated over and over again. A continuous shifting of points takes place along a line always identical to itself. This cradlelike movement back and forth between the same points has its analogue in the movements of Riefenstahl's camera. The repetitive structure of her photographic technique is especially evident in the marching scenes toward the end of the film, scenes in which she continuously moves away from and returns to a few privileged angles of vision (we are above and behind the lines of marchers, or to the side of Hitler's car watching from under his outstretched arms). The pseudomobility of these cradling movements seduces us into a hypnotically sensual fascination with repetition. The movements of Riefenstahl's camera suggest that she is seeking to dominate a spectacle which has in fact already seduced her. The camera's repetitious mobility in *Triumph of the Will* reflects — and supports — the immobilizing mobility of Nazism's military theatrics.[22]

A considerable number of Assyrian reliefs depict scenes of soldiers marching off to war, of the king's subjects or prisoners lined up in submissive poses, and of hunters returning home with their dead prey on their shoulders. In important respects, all these scenes are similar to the military march. Numerous human figures engaged in the same activity, moving (or looking) in the same direction, create a powerful impression of homogeneity, of a single line of force. Critics frequently deplore this processional side of Assyrian art — just as they deplore the violence in the palace reliefs. But objections to all the lined-up prisoners and soldiers are, it seems to us, as ill-founded as the objections to violence. They are based, in both instances, on narrative readings of the palace reliefs, readings made largely irrelevant by the Assyrian sculptors' subversion of narrative in their treatment of both physical violence and the processions of war and of hunting.

The military march could be thought of as a simplified display of certain narrative principles. The march abstracts from any narrative content the formal narrative principle of an ordered succession or unfolding, and in so doing it suggests that the pleasure of following a narrative lies less in the story being told than in the security of being passively carried along by an unfolding order. In most literary narratives — especially in the modern novel, which is a comparatively loose narrative form — there are always (unrealized) threats to this unfolding order. Most dramatically, the heroes and heroines of nineteenth-century realistic fiction frequently represent disruptive possibilities within that fiction. Such figures as Melville's Ahab, Dostoevski's Prince Myshkin, Stendhal's Fabrice del Dongo, and even Henry James's Milly Theale and George Eliot's Dorothea Brooke remain unexplained within the novelistic worlds which would not interest us without them but which are also unable to account for their natures. The protagonist of realistic fiction is often outside the orders of intelligibility which make realistic fiction possible. Consequently, he or she is expelled from the novel, usually in sacrificial fashion — as if the heroes and heroines of realistic fiction were the necessary scapegoats by which these novelists (and perhaps their society) exorcised from their midst a seductively but dangerously disruptive, incoherent presence.

The *process* of expulsion is the life of the novel. Thus particular narrative textures are always differential textures, and the suspense generated by narrative could be defined as an uncertainty about how and when differences will be resolved. Obviously, we do not mean that narratives work toward a literal reduction of diversity to sameness. In the realistic novel, for example, the resolution of tension is not accompanied by the absorption of individual characters into a kind of collective novelistic spirit. But the resolutions toward which most narrative works (or, as the narratologists have put it, the equilibrium to which they return after passing through a state of disequilibrium) do depend on a reduction of difference, or on a dialectical union of antagonistic forces (a union which dissipates much of the antagonism). In realistic fiction, differences are absorbed into the novel's order of intelligibility, and, as we suggested a moment ago, figures who resist this absorption into a community of meaning are the ambiguously heroic victims of catastrophe in the realistic novel.

The homogenizing of the realistic novelist's world frequently takes the form of a merging of various points of view into a single point of view. The fundamental drama in Jane Austen's fiction, for example, is almost always the closing of the gap between the "right" perspective on the world and certain interesting but erroneous perspectives. Elisabeth Bennett and Darcy in *Pride and Prejudice,* Emma in the novel to which she gives her name, and Edmond in *Mansfield Park* are all guilty of wrong interpretations. The right interpretations are — explicitly or implicitly — present in the novel from the very start. In *Mansfield Park,* Fanny Price judges everyone else correctly; in *Emma,* the right judgments are incorporated into the narrative perspective and they create a small but crucial ironic distance between Jane Austen's voice and Emma's voice. The closing of the gap resolves these narrative tensions; it is also the precondition of happy marriages and, more generally, of life in society. Social viability in Jane Austen's fiction requires the homogenizing of points of view. As *Mansfield Park* in particular suggests, the survival of a principled social life depends on shared judgments of behavior. The interpretive system developed in Austen's novels monitors self-expression and forestalls theatricalizing impulses which threaten to expand the self beyond the range of systematic understanding.

In the later James and in Proust, the merging of points of view takes a much more radical form. Instead of the more or less believable process by which clearly differentiated characters reach certain moral agreements, we find in Proust and in James a partial breakdown of those very differences which constitute character itself in realistic fiction. Repetitions of being are more visible in *Remembrance of Things Past* than in Stendhal or Dickens. Novelistic character is exposed, in an exceptionally transparent way, as the novelist's self-projection. Just beneath the impressively diversified surfaces of being in Proust's world, we find an ontological community in which the principal figures all reenact the narrator's obsessional system. In Proust and in James, the novel moves toward allegory, that is, toward the transformation of socially and psychologically distinct human beings into the emblematic tokens or props of a monologue. In James's *The Wings of the Dove,* this en-

closing of other people within a single circle of being becomes almost super-
natural. By the end of the novel, Merton Densher is living entirely within
the orbit of the dead, dovelike Milly Theale. In a sense, he *is* Milly, for
she has become little more than a spiritual choice, and his allegiance to her
is, novelistically, the substitution of an inexpressible, nonfrictional sameness of being for the frictional differences which the novel works to eliminate,
but without which the novel itself dies.[23]

The sense-making orders of narrative accommodate differences only to
the extent that difference does not explode a structural frame. That is, they
accommodate differences fundamentally homogenous with the terms within
their own enclosures of sense. In such systems of order, oppositions are dialectical: their frictional contact produces compromises and syntheses which
reduce or even eliminate the friction. Radically heterogeneous differences,
on the other hand, resist fusions of any sort. They do not produce a new
term which impoverishes them by expressing only what they have in common. Rather, as we have seen in Assyrian art, such differences act on one
another merely by coexisting; when they are put into relation with one
another, they immediately produce new forms (new differential elements)
which remove us from the original relation and themselves initiate further
removals into an ever expanding field of difference.

The ideally executed military parade homogenizes being with a perfec-
tion of which literary narratives are incapable. The order of the parade is
simultaneously unfolding and already achieved. Literary narratives may succeed in mastering differences, but the very process of mastery requires a
certain accommodation of differences. Military marches, on the other hand,
give us the order without the process; or more exactly, they create the illusion of a *detemporalized process*. In parades, the ideal goal of narrative ordering occupies the narrative line itself; we watch a "progression" of identical
elements.

The Assyrian sculptors might easily have produced a similar effect. Indeed, a pictorial representation of marches or lines of people lends itself better
to a detemporalizing intent than the actual events represented. In sculpture
and painting, the unfurling of exactly identical elements is rendered by the
simultaneous presence of all those elements. Time is spatialized, and we
can seize the entire unchanging order of marching warriors or lined-up
prisoners in a single glance. But the Assyrians, in spite of their obvious taste
for this sort of scene, have numerous strategies which block any such uni-

tary perception. The members of an embassy to Ashurbanipal from Urartu in Figure 42 are differentiated not only by their having or not having a beard; there are also the slightly different angles at which their swords hang from their sides, as well as the variations among their hands and even the different ways in which the same headdress is being worn by the two bearded men to the right. The reader may already have been struck by this art of differentiation in our very first photograph of a scene from the palace reliefs. In Figure 2 (see page 5), the Elamite subjects lined up to greet their King Ummanigash on his arrival at Madaktu would at first seem designed to produce a powerful narrative effect: the worshipful poses repeatedly lead us to the standing figure of the king. But precisely because of details similar to those just noted in Figure 42, we are stopped in our narrative reading of these adoring subjects and are forced to pay more attention to the differences among them than to the comparatively insignificant if "climactic" representations of the king to the left. The numerous versions of lined-up human figures in the Assyrian palace reliefs almost always have an effect opposite to that of parades or military marches; indeed, the repetitions in these scenes appear to be pretexts for an artful play of variations within a group of similar elements.

But if no two faces in the relief are ever the same, the differences do not express different characters. The Assyrians frequently render differences with a naturalistic scruple usually associated with psychological intentions. The highly individualized heads in Roman sculpture, for example, are portraits of particular personalities. If we think of a psychologically nonexpressive figurative art, we are likely to take classical Greek sculpture as our example. The Greeks give us recognizable but idealized human figures, but ones insufficiently individualized to be psychologically informative. We feel comfortable with the alternative best exemplified in Greek and Roman sculpture: between the subordination of the personal and the idiosyncratic to an idealized view of the human figure on the one hand, and on the other, the triumph of the individual over the type in a richly psychological art.

But the Assyrians give us something outside this alternative: a realistic art in which the human body is individualized but nonexpressive. There

Figure 42: Ashurbanipal receives an embassy from Urartu at Arbela. *From the South West Palace at Nimrud.*

Figure 42

is an impressive range of facial types in Figure 43, but they do not have the effect of substituting a more "refined" psychological interest for the grosser narrative design of glorifying the king. (Psychology would not in any case subvert narrative; it merely creates more sophisticated narratives.) The faces in Assyrian sculpture are blank or bland; a vague smile is the strongest expressive element in the representation in Figure 43 of the Elamite king's worshipful subjects. In a sense, critics are right to speak of the palace reliefs as stereotypic; where they are wrong is to take this observation as a self-evident condemnation. Given the extraordinary capacity for visual differentiations which the Assyrians show in their art, it seems to us presumptuous to conclude that they are unable to imagine psychological differences. Or rather, it is a presumption typical of our culture to give the psychological imagination priority over other ways of imagining differences. The Assyrians never use a human face to tell a psychological story. They do of course use human figures as semiotic markers, as, for example, indications of hierarchical importance or insignificance. But this is not the same thing as the use of the body (and especially of the face) for the purposes of individualizing a figure psychologically. In a sense, faces interest the Assyrians for their sheer visibility, not for any presumed depth. What strikes us as an extraordinary respect for all the appearances in the universe — human as well as nonhuman — leads them to represent an incredible variety of volumes in human bodies rather than the necessarily limited signs of a hypothetical and constraining human nature.

The clear difference between the two faces in Figure 44 (part of the Return From the Hunt) is entirely a difference of shapes and volumes. And perhaps because we can read no feelings on these faces, the differences themselves seem part of a continuous surface. There is no psychological delineation intended to make us find one face more interesting than another, and as a result we see human beings as a community of impressively diversified forms. In twentieth-century art, Picasso has made us familiar with this geometric solidarity among men and women. Like the Assyrians, he suspends those stories about feeling which narrativize human life, which create the subordinations and tensions from which separations (rather than difference) spring.

Figure 43: The Elamite King Ummanigash is greeted on his arrival at Madaktu. (Detail of Figure 2.) *From the South West Palace at Nineveh.*

Figure 43

The temptation of exact repetition seems, astonishingly, to act as a powerful stimulus to the Assyrians' imagination of differences. Not only do they use lines of human figures in order to prevent us from seeing those figures *as* lines of identical elements; they also play, in a variety of contexts, with at least two versions of the same object or activity. The palace reliefs suggest a compulsive fascination with these double images. Almost every aspect of Figure 45 is juxtaposed with a near repetition of itself: the men's heads and legs, their outstretched arms, and their shields and swords. And yet, curiously enough, our attention is perhaps most powerfully solicited by a form which, while repeating certain other forms, is also distinctly different from them: the circle of the lion's tail. And this dramatic example of difference within repetition should lead us to notice less obvious differences elsewhere: between the men's hats and heads as well as between the shapes of the two legs to the left, in the different angles of their extended arms, and between the two shields, only one of which is complete. (Strictly speaking, the lower shield is not a circle: the bottom part of the top shield becomes its upper boundary, a boundary which dips into a position nearly parallel with the bottom curve of the bottom shield.)

Repetition and difference are combined with even greater subtlety in the beautiful fragment represented in Figure 46. There are three sets of paired images here: the huntsmen's heads, the lion's paws, and the two hands roughly in the same position. But this order is also thwarted by the peculiar dissonances between the elements of each couple. The animal's paws move away from each other, and the upper paw is parallel not to its mate but to the tail draped over the shoulder of the man to the left. Also, which hand is the hand to the right really paired with? It lies on the lion's body in a position similar to that of the vertical hand to the left, and yet its diagonal shape makes it appear to be an extension of the arm rising diagonally toward it from the lower left. As is frequently the case in the palace reliefs, repetition gives rise to doubt or puzzlement in the spectator. One proceeds from A to its repetition in A¹, but the latter contains a difference which makes us check the model by returning to A. *Repetition in Assyrian sculpture makes repeti-*

Figure 44: Return from the hunt. *From the North Palace of Ashurbanipal at Nineveh.*
Figure 45: King Ashurnasirpal hunts lions from his chariot. *From the North West Palace at Nimrud.* **Figure 46:** Return from the hunt. *From the North Palace of Ashurbanipal at Nineveh.*

Figure 45

Figure 46

tion itself problematic. It appears to provide the strongest elements of order in our visual field, whereas in fact it initiates an inconclusive movement of perceptual verification on our part between the repeated terms.

In Figure 46, the visual mobility thus created by insistent but inexact repetition is increased by the multidirectional aspect of the scene. Almost all its elements are pointing somewhere, but they point in a dizzying variety of directions: the huntsmen's eyes straight to the right, one hand vertically down, another diagonally down, and the third diagonally upward, one paw horizontally to the left and resting on the tail which, like the other paw, directs us upward and to the left. There is a curious contrast between the hunters' stolid faces and this orgy of implied or solicited movement. A kind of explosive centrifugal force is contained by the expressionless, heavy volumes of these two faces. That force is also somewhat "pacified" by the enclosed empty space at the center of the scene, a space which relieves the agitated complexity of the forms surrounding it. At the same time, in helping us to recognize and to sort out the cues in the dense parts of the scene, the emptiness of this small central field indirectly serves the cause of mobility by clarifying the space in which all those cues compete for our attention.

Multidirectional movement frequently frustrates our impulse to give a narrative reading of the scenes in Assyrian sculpture. The progress of the four figures in Figure 48 is both negated and accentuated by the first man's arm and the third man's head pointing away from the direction in which they appear to be swiftly walking. On the one hand, it is the negation of the forward movement which makes us feel the thrust of that movement; the contravening gesture mobilizes the scene, thereby working against the nonkinetic nature of bas-relief. But the conflicting movement also keeps the principal movement from being completed. Narrative goals are subverted before they are reached, and our visual pleasure lies not in being carried along in one direction toward a central point of interest, but rather in being submitted to the repeated interruptions of uncompleted movements. Figure 49 shows how marvelously complex these kinetic messages can be. The arms

Figure 47: Ashurbanipal in his chariot shooting lions. (Detail of Figure 19.) *From the North Palace of Ashurbanipal at Nineveh.* **Figure 48:** Spectators (of the royal lion hunt) on a mound. *From the North Palace of Ashurbanipal at Nineveh.* **Figure 49:** Ashurbanipal receives an embassy from Urartu at Arbela. *From the South West Palace at Nineveh.*

Figure 47

Figure 48

Figure 49

of these figures from a scene representing Ashurbanipal receiving an embassy from Urartu at Arbela are going in so many directions that we hardly know where to look. The eye registers more than it can focus on, and the rapidity of its movements undermines visual stability.

The effect in these scenes is not unlike that of dance, for all the obvious differences between the two art forms. We are thinking especially of those moments in a Balanchine ballet when dancers interrupt the line of movement in order to begin a movement in another direction. Such moments can perhaps best be understood in terms of the subversive nature of Balanchine's relation to the idiom of classical ballet. He was of course totally absorbed in that idiom. He saw the positions and movements of classical dance as an inventory of the human body's potential gestures and shapes, and he therefore composed ballets which explore those potentialities instead of subordinating them to the expressive needs of a dramatic spectacle. But to say this is to suggest the complicated nature of Balanchine's relation to classical ballet. Even in such great works as *Swan Lake* and *Sleeping Beauty,* the purely physical nature of dance is somewhat disguised by a subordination of the dancers' bodies to their roles. It is as if the sublimating processes operable in all art produced a particularly severe code of decorum in ballet. The body is put on display, but it is also devalued: human expressiveness is separated from the body's movements, or at the very least these movements are immediately translatable into emotions. "Pure dance" in classical ballet frequently stops the show, and not merely in the sense of provoking long spells of applause from the audience. It is a *divertissement:* it diverts us from the story, which is suspended while the dancers display their virtuosity. With notable exceptions (such as a good part of the *pas de deux* in the second act of *Swan Lake*), we move between expressive gesture and musicalized gymnastics in classical ballet. The assumption is that emotion exists somewhere prior to the dance; it must therefore be designated through pantomime, or referred to by the limited number of dance movements which can be easily interpreted because they resemble the conventionalized signs of emotion in social life.

Choreographic invention in the narrative ballets of the classical repertory is somewhat constrained by this double preoccupation with emotionally significant movement and the coherence of a complete dramatic spectacle. It is the genius of Balanchine to have separated the dramatic aspect of dance from the theatrical conventions of traditional theater (a complete story and intelligible characters), and to have demonstrated the ways in which move-

ment produces emotion instead of merely reflecting it. In such great Balanchine pieces as *Agon, Violin Concerto,* and *Duo Concertant* (all to Stravinsky
scores), e-motion is, quite properly, what emerges from motion. Balanchine's
work therefore suggests that emotion is not a state symbolized by movement; rather, it is equivalent to the movements we make or fantasize among
perceived forms. We might recall Freud's definition of desire not as a static
inner condition, but rather as the fantasy-movement designed to re-create
a satisfying perceptual experience. We are of course not saying that a Balanchine ballet reproduces or even resembles psychic movements of desire. But
his erotic *pas de deux* do give us, within the choreographic medium, *figures*
of desire: to be moved by them is to recognize that emotion is always a question of formal agitations. And these agitations, far from producing the narrative inevitabilities of classical ballet and classical theater, involve continuous
changes of direction, a continuous thwarting—as in the Assyrian palace
reliefs—of the impulse to complete movement, to freeze representations into
the finality of a motionless tableau.

The Shifting Line
of Sensual Experience

The visual mobility which Assyrian sculpture promotes could be taken as the model for a nonclimactic sensuality. In our remarks on the Marquis de Sade, we spoke of a narrative form of sexuality, a sexuality in which the orgasmic climax closes an incident of desire. Sade translates into scenarios of literal violence the calculated organization of erotic activity in view of explosive culminations. His work illustrates the relation between a commitment to narrativity and a commitment to certain types of pleasure. Sade thereby proposes that the life of the body does not merely happen; we cultivate, organize, dismiss, or concentrate on sensations just as we order our thoughts and dismiss or linger over spectacles in the external world. The Assyrians decenter their representations and keep our attention constantly on the move; they plunge us into a network of shifting relations which destabilize narrative structures. But what exactly is this mobility? What sorts of pleasures can it oppose to the powerful sensations which accompany climactic meanings and climactic releases?

A frequent configuration in the palace reliefs is that of two parallel lines fairly close to each other, and, at some distance, another set of lines parallel to the first two. This is another example of the Assyrians' daring use of elements ideally suited to produce static effects (such as circles and processions) in order to produce the opposite effect of disruptive mobility. Parallel lines create an order based on identical repetition. To read two parallel lines on a flat surface is to read the space between them as a space always identical to itself.[24] Parallel lines can be used to reinforce narrative effects in painting and sculpture merely by providing the frame which focuses our attention on centers of narrative interest. The signs of exasperation with these framing effects in modern painting (such as the use of irregularly shaped canvases, or the tracing of a mangled or incomplete frame within the painting itself) could be thought of as strategies designed to prevent this focusing on centers, to destructure and disseminate the spectator's interest.[25]

In Figure 50, it is the line of the bowstring, nearly parallel to the line of the spears, which helps the Assyrian sculptors to decenter our attention. For in crossing the space between the two spears and the bowstring, we are drawn away both from the anecdotal violence accentuated by the spears (and the two hands) *and,* to the extent that the bowstring moves us toward the scene to the left, from the stabilizing order of parallel lines themselves. As we can see if we re-place this fragment with the larger scene shown in Figure 51 (both of which, like Figures 36 and 47, are fragments of Figure 19; see pages 30, 77, and 99), the parallelism of the two spears and the bowstring should initiate a continuous movement between the scene to the right and the scene to the left. The empty space within the parallelogram is thus an extremely important part of the scene; our eye is always crossing this space in order to follow the contradictory cues on its edges. It leads us to terminal points which are in fact anything but terminal, which continuously send us back across the space between them. We have repeatedly traced multidirectional movements in Assyrian sculpture which interrupt or block our narrative reading of scenes. Figure 51 can help us to refine the notion of mobility which has been central to this discussion. We now wish to suggest that *the spectator's pleasure in following all the cues in Assyrian sculpture which displace his or her interest and attention is less in the variety of scenes which are thereby taken in than in the very tension of the displacing movement itself.*

In establishing these continuously dismissed and displaced relational terms, the viewer experiences a pleasure akin to the pleasure of desire. We spoke earlier of desire as a pleasurable movement toward an absent (and, in a nonfetishistic theory of desire, unlocatable) source of satisfaction. The pleasure of desire is inseparable from the tension created by the lack in desire. Desire constitutes a mobile and indeterminate sensuality. It is never quite focused on its "object" (which is both present and absent in the rich but insubstantial images of desiring fantasy); and the incomplete pleasures of desire, incapable by definition of filling the lack in desire, stimulate the productive restlessness of fantasies always on the move. In the visual mobility which we have been describing in connection with the Assyrian palace reliefs, the spectator moves between two forms with a residual impression of the first form and in anticipation of the second. The latter will, presumably, "complete" the former by establishing a structurally intelligible relation

---

Figures 50 and 51: Ashurbanipal in his chariot shooting lions. (Details of Figure 19.) *From the North Palace of Ashurbanipal at Nineveh.*

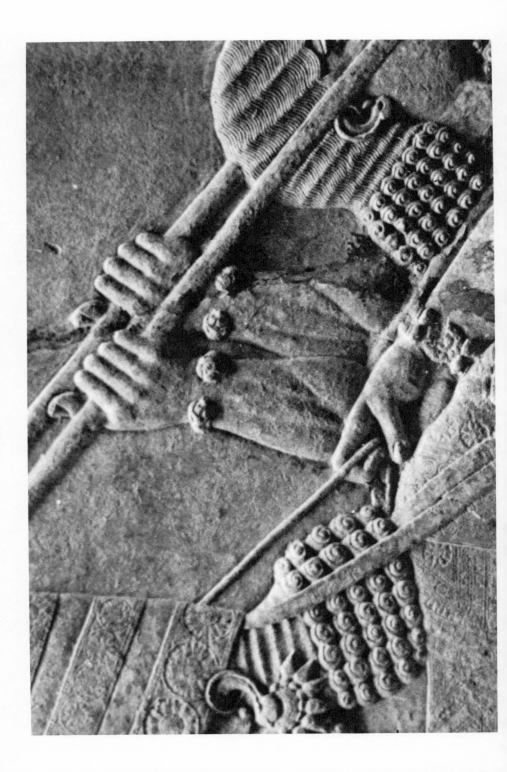

Figure 51

with it. But, as we have seen, the second form also initiates departures toward other forms. This constant mobility leads us to postulate an esthetic pleasure brought about not by esthetic objects but by the spaces between their constituent parts. We may define this pleasure as an agitated crossing of the intervals which separate forms. Assyrian art is a lesson in *interstitial sensuality.*[26]

The sensuality we refer to is by no means an exclusively esthetic phenomenon; it is crucial, we believe, to actual sexual contact. Bodies moving in sex never touch all over all the time; sex is not a massage in which surfaces would be totally covered. Sexual experience could therefore be thought of in terms of the multiple intervals during which different parts of the bodies' surfaces are *not* in contact, but are rather between two instants of contact. This may be a physical analogue of the psychic phenomenon of desire: various parts of one body travel along another body with both the "imprints" of pleasures already felt and the "expectation" of those pleasures being repeated.

On the one hand, desiring fantasy works toward an immobilizing wholeness; it aims at a stable representation which would end (the irritation of) desire. Fantasy is inescapably mimetic; it seeks to capture and to replay images. But desiring fantasy is also always an approximation which, moreover, disturbs the self's equilibrium. The immobilizing intent of desire is ruined by this double freakishness: the fantasies of desire are intrinsically off-mark (and therefore nonclimactic), and the shattering excitement which they generate makes it impossible to locate the source of excitement. *The masochistic excitement which perhaps initiates us to sexuality can therefore be exploited not as the goal of representation, but rather as a psychic "technique" for destabilizing representation and maintaining mobility.* Desiring fantasy seeks to totalize a satisfying scene at the same time that its very nature is to move among the scattered (and shattered) elements of deconstructed scenes. The excitements of desire and of sexual contact can therefore be intervallic or interstitial: between the images of desire, between touching and nontouching. In sex, we partly experience our own body and the other's body as related but nontotalized bits and pieces. Intermittent touch shatters the body's wholeness and produces pleasures dependent on disseminated, unstructured bodily surfaces. Thus the Assyrian palace reliefs, which are of course not "about" sexuality at all, can nonetheless help us to define a sensuality in which neither beginnings nor endings are assigned to relations and in which differences proliferate and meet without being transcended.

The Shifting Line of Sensual Experience

An insistently narrative sexuality, on the other hand, implicitly denies the pleasures of mobile nontouching. It insists on one direction and one goal; pleasure increases in intensity and is finally concentrated (and consummated) at a single point on the body's surface. This is the sexuality of Fellini's Casanova, a sexuality in which the movement preceding orgasm is a repetitious thrusting designed to precipitate the coming of the end. Motion here is madly frictional, along a "straight line" of pleasure, and always in the same place; the time before the explosive climax is merely one of painful physical suspense. Casanovian sex, for all its insane emphasis on the orgasm (or rather, because of it), is especially vulnerable to impotence. A man's inability to have an orgasm may be due to a refusal to change directions: the male orgasm is, in a sense, a sudden shift in the dynamics of sex, a giving up of willful, controlled movements in order to allow himself to be carried away by the involuntary movements of a climactic release. Perhaps a proper understanding of the male orgasm would prevent us from treating it as a *definitive* climax. The instant of orgasm is a residual thrusting toward climax which takes place simultaneously with a spasmodic release of tension. One must abandon oneself to a change of direction, actively accept a certain passivity, and a refusal to do that can mean an inability to stop going *toward* the climax, to take the other direction inherent in reaching a climax.[27] The orgasm itself can therefore instruct us not to place it at the summit of sexuality, but to experiment with "placing" it at various points along an irregular, always shifting line of sensual experience.

The Restlessness of Desire

We have been opposing a disruptive mobility of attention to the narrative immobilization of privileged scenes. In our description of a perceptual agitation which continuously relocates our attention and destabilizes perceptual orders, many readers will undoubtedly have recognized characteristics attributed by Freud to the "primary process." We should, however, say at once that we do not intend to suggest an equivalence between the displaced yet guided attention encouraged by the palace reliefs and the displacements of the primary process. In its pure, and purely hypothetical, state, the latter would be dysfunctional; it could not be "salvaged" for esthetic or moral purposes. Nonetheless, it has long been felt that the mode of mental activity which Freud labeled the primary process is somehow relevant to the specificity of artistic invention.[28] We share this view, realizing that the "somehow" is immensely problematic. We do not reopen an old discussion in order to suggest, as others have, that psychic censorship is relaxed in art and that, as a result, the primary process can emerge from the unconscious and determine much of the organization of artistic materials. Rather, we will be moving toward a view of the primary process which will allow us to dispense with such psychic melodramas. The primary process is always *in* the process which presumably replaces it. And conversely, its own existence is perhaps inseparable from the operations which continuously suppress it. We will argue this position by following a double operation in Freud's own description of the primary process: his simultaneous confirmation and denial of the significance of that process as delineating the movements of all desiring fantasy.

As early as the *Project For a Scientific Psychology* (1895), Freud had speculated on a type of mental activity radically different from the processes of thought and feeling studied by classical psychology. Five years later, in the extraordinary section on "The Psychology of the Dream-Processes" (Chapter 7) in *The Interpretation of Dreams,* Freud proposed a distinction which has remained the cornerstone of psychoanalytic thought and practice. Working

110

with dreams allowed Freud to refine the biological speculations of the *Project* into a theory of the psychic functions served by different modes of mental activity. He came to distinguish between the manifest content of a dream (the uninterpreted descriptions of their dreams which patients give to their analysts),[29] and a dream's latent content (its hidden meaning). The latter includes everything which has been uncovered through analysis of the dream: residues from the previous day's experience, the dreamer's associations, and, most significantly, a repressed wishful impulse from the dreamer's past which has managed to transfer itself onto the day's residues. Once this latent content has been revealed through interpretation, the dreamer and the analyst possess an adequate and coherent expression of the wish which the dream seeks to fulfill; that is, an expression of the dream's sense. But the dream itself offers no such coherent expression of its own *raison d'être;* what the dream is saying can be made intelligible only through interpretation. Between the dream's origin and its explanation, there is, then, a process of distortion. Freud calls this process the dream-work, and its effect is to make the latent content, or what Freud also calls the dream-thoughts, virtually unreadable.

In studying his patients' dreams (and his own), and having noticed startling resemblances between dream structures and the structures of certain neurotic symptoms (especially in hysteria), Freud was able to abstract the general characteristics of the dream-work and to assert the fundamental intelligibility of both dreams and neurotic symptoms. But there is a profound ambivalence in his discussion of the dream-work. On the one hand, he seems to be describing nothing more than the rules by which rational dream-thoughts are disguised and distorted. This appears to be the case with condensation and displacement. As a result of condensation, for example, ". . . the intensity of a whole train of thought may eventually be concentrated in a single ideational element" (SE, 5:595). There are, originally, several different chains of association in the dream-thoughts; the dream-work can condense all the elements of these associative chains, often in confusing fashion, into a single representation. Similarly, in displacement there is a shift in the "real" affective intensities being expressed in the dream: a strong affect attached in the dream-thought to one figure moves to another, insignificant figure. Interpretation consists in re-placing the displaced affect, in putting it back where it presumably belongs.

Condensation and displacement would be the signs of a formalistic game by which certain thoughts (or, more precisely, the wishes fulfilled in dreams) were sufficiently scrambled so that they can slip into consciousness. Freud explains this as a compromise effected by censorship: certain inadmissible contents of the mind can gain admission to consciousness only if they can no longer be recognized by consciousness. From this perspective, condensation and displacement serve a regulatory instance (censorship) which, by definition, belongs to the conscious or preconscious mind.[30] The distortions of the dream-work would therefore not designate an area of the mind (or a mode of "thinking") to which the dream-thought originally belonged; instead, these distortions are *imposed on* the dream-thought as the very condition of its joining the more familiar contents and processes of the mind.

In a sense, condensation and displacement would not be too different from another characteristic of the dream-work, the "secondary revision" by which the elements of a dream are, as it were, reviewed for intelligibility, made into something like the relatively coherent scenario of a daydream. In all these cases, the dream-work would appear to be a function of consciousness, or at least of an agency which determines how and if thoughts and feelings may enter consciousness. In spite of the obvious differences between transformations designed to make a dream more coherent and other transformations designed to mislead us as to what the dream is really saying, condensation, displacement, and secondary revision all appear to be the effects of a certain virtuosity of reason which, far from introducing us to other mental areas or other mental processes, merely cosmeticizes the dream-thought so that it may appear on the stage of a sleeping, but by no means uncritical consciousness.

But this is clearly not what Freud finds most interesting in his description of the dream-work's characteristics. We find in *The Interpretation of Dreams* a curious and immensely productive uncertainty about how to "place" condensation and displacement in the human mind. For it is on the basis of a process which makes dream-thoughts fit for consciousness that Freud also infers the existence of a process alien to the conscious mind, the process which governs the operations of the unconscious. In describing the activities of censorship, Freud discovers a mode of mental activity which is more general than the dream-work and which, unlike the dream-work, is in no way involved in regulating the contents of consciousness.

Considered along with another important feature of the dream-work, displacement and condensation can be taken as distinctive operations of the unconscious itself. We are thinking of the "considerations of representability" peculiar to dreams and which require that the most abstract meanings of a dream be expressed through images. Dream-thoughts enter dreams along a path of regression to a visual mode of expression. Freud at first explains this in topographical terms: the excitation in dreams "moves in a *backward* direction. Instead of being transmitted toward the *motor* end of the [psychic] apparatus it moves toward the *sensory* end and finally reaches the perceptual system" (SE, 5:542). Unable to be satisfied through appropriate physical movements, the motivating desire in a dream is fulfilled in a hallucinatory mode, that is, in the visual imagery of a dream. But this hallucinatory substitute for motor activity is also a temporal regression. The wishes expressed in dream-thoughts, and which analysis uncovers, are unconscious wishes from childhood which alone provide the motive power for the dream's construction. As a result of this regression, ideas are transformed into pictures, and in a sense the dream-thought returns to its own raw material when it goes back to the perceptual memory-traces which express a repressed but now partially revived wish. Thus, given the role played by infantile experiences and fantasies in dreams, Freud proposes that

> . . . the transformation of thoughts into visual images may be in part the result of the attraction which memories couched in visual form and eager for revival bring to bear upon thoughts cut off from consciousness and struggling to find expression. On this view a dream might be described as *a substitute for an infantile scene modified by being transferred on to a recent experience.* The infantile scene is unable to bring about its own revival and has to be content with returning as a dream (SE, 5:546).

Part of the dream-work's camouflaging activity therefore consists in returning the wish expressed in the dream to its original mode of expression. The most authentic expression of that wish serves as its most effective disguise.

The temporally regressive nature of dreams is verified in analysis when the dreamer associates images of a dream with a remembered or fantasized scene from childhood. And the revival of memory-traces through dream analysis suggests that censorship, far from initiating the peculiar operations of the dream-work, actually borrows them from an "instance" of mind in which, for example, wishes and thoughts exist in scenic terms. Censorship does not invent the forms in which the dream-thoughts become admissible to consciousness; rather, it uses forms of expression which already exist in the mind and in which consciousness will, presumably, be unable to detect the offensive dream-thought. This distinction is crucial, for it allows us to move from a consideration of the dream-work's operations as purely strategic to a view of those operations as constituting a distinct mode of mental activity. Indeed, it is precisely by detaching the characteristics of the dream-work from their defensive function that Freud is able to begin a description of the unconscious. The strategic use of condensation and displacement in a dream does not exhaust their ontological status. The dream-thought, having been neglected or suppressed by consciousness, comes under the sway of other mental processes, processes of which it gives a somewhat truncated version when it uses them to produce a dream.

The mechanism of displacement in dreams allows Freud to formulate the most distinctive feature of the primary process. After summarizing "some of the most striking of the abnormal processes to which the dream-thoughts, previously constructed on rational lines, are subjected in the course of the dream-work," Freud writes, in Chapter 7 of *The Interpretation of Dreams:* "It will be seen that the chief characteristic of these processes is that the whole stress is laid upon making the cathecting energy mobile and capable of discharge; the content and the proper meaning of the psychical elements to which the cathexes are attached are treated as of little consequence." A couple of pages later, this mobility will be posited as the major difference between two mental systems: "I therefore postulate that for the sake of efficiency the second system succeeds in retaining the major part of its cathexes of energy in a state of quiescence and in employing only a small part of displacement. . . . The activity of the *first* system is directed toward securing the *free discharge* of the quantities of excitation, while the second system, by means of the cathexes emanating from it, succeeds in *inhibiting* this discharge and in transforming the cathexis into a quiescent one, no doubt with a simultaneous raising of its level" (SE, 5:596–97, 599).

Now the very presence of psychic energy seems to be equivalent, for Freud, to the presence of a wish. (Our psychic apparatus, Freud writes in *The Interpretation of Dreams,* can be set in motion only by a wish [SE, 5:567].) Psychic energy seeking to discharge itself is a wish seeking to be fulfilled. But when Freud speaks of the desiring energy which constitutes the unconscious, he also asserts that this energy "can never become an object of consciousness — only the idea that represents the instinct can" (SE, 14:177). That is, we know the instinctual desiring energy of life only as the fantasmatic scenarios of particular desires. The contents of the unconscious are therefore not currents of "pure" instinctual or desiring energy, but rather the representations by which desire "stages" its fulfillment. One might take this argument a step further: there is no energy prior to the representations

of desire, an energy which would, as it were, move around trying on different fantasies for satisfaction. Rather, we suggest that *desiring energy is contem-
poraneous with its representation in the human psyche, and that the very deployment
of a fantasy is a mental agitation which scrambles its own terms and initiates other,
equally precarious fantasmatic events.* Displacement in this sense would be a kind
of relational frenzy. Instead of imagining a stable set of discrete representations with currents of energy traveling among them, we should perhaps think
of displacement as a continuous modification of the representations themselves.

Freud speaks of the ease with which intensities can be transferred in the
unconscious from one group of images to another. The factors which limit
such transfers in the conscious mind are apparently inoperative in the unconscious: the processes of the latter system are not ordered chronologically
(and so temporal distinctions are not respected), they are not restricted by
a sense of reality (and can therefore give free rein to the pleasure principle),
and logical contradictions never prevent ideas from coming together. What
we should try to imagine is a "system" in constant disintegration and re-
formation as a result of the uninhibited and ever-changing relations among
its elements. And these relations would be the consequence of the very nature of a desiring fantasy. Each unconscious representation magnetizes the
field in which it occurs; it annexes adjacent elements for its own scenario,
but the process of repeated annexations disrupts all scenarios. The psychic
ébranlement, or shattering of stable equilibriums which, for Laplanche, *is* fantasy, would include a disruptive shifting around of the elements which constitute fantasy. Thus energy would not move *from* one representation *to*
another; rather, desiring energy would *be* the tendency of all unconscious
representations to multiply themselves by establishing relations with adjacent or associated images. The energy of desiring fantasy, incapable of ever
being wholly discharged, is always diversifying fantasy configurations.

Along with these shifting figures, we would also have uneven distribu-
tions of intensity. All fantasies are perhaps immediately decentered by the
heterogeneous associations between their constituent parts and a surrounding field, and this decentering of a desiring impulse is equivalent to reduc-
tions and relocations of quantities of energy. "The cathectic intensities in
the unconscious are much more mobile," Freud writes in his 1915 essay on
"The Unconscious." "By the process of *displacement* one idea may surrender
to another its whole quota of cathexis; by the process of *condensation* it may

115

appropriate the whole cathexis of several other ideas" (SE, 14:186). Thus, displacement and condensation, far from having only the defensive function assigned to them in dreams, could be thought of as attributes inherent in unconscious fantasy processes. They are what happens in the *ébranlement* of fantasy; that is, they describe the destabilizing, dislocating nature of fantasy. Fantasy is unbound energy, and another way of saying this is that fantasies are intrinsically unstable representations. In the terms used most frequently in this study, desiring fantasy is displaced fantasy, and *displacement is nonnarrative representation.*

Narrative orders, on the other hand, are a triumph of the conscious mind. In *The Interpretation of Dreams,* Freud refers to another system, governed by the secondary process, a system responsible for the activities most familiar to us and to which pre-Freudian psychology had addressed itself: reasoning, judgment, attention, and will. The secondary process binds energy. We have just said that free energy should be understood not only as energy seeking a total, immediate discharge, but also as shifting intensities among shifting unconscious representations. Analogously, the secondary process does not simply prevent an impulse from being discharged in motor activities; it also creates stable representations within the mind. Bound energy would be equivalent to a relational stability among mental representations, and relations are stabilized by being limited. Bound energy is obviously a precondition both of logical, concentrated thought and of the effective manipulation of objects in the external world. Knowledge depends on the ability to arrive at conclusions, and conclusions can be reached only if the terms of our thoughts and the relations among them remain relatively constant. In rational processes, displacement is shifted from ideas or images to the logical moves which treat ideas or images as objects. Logic works with a kind of investigatory mobility as a result of which we can formulate certain orders and impose them on reality.

In *The Interpretation of Dreams,* Freud makes a distinction which will not recur in his work but which we find indispensable for an understanding of how the secondary process differs from the primary process: the distinction between perceptual identity and thought identity. The primary process seeks to reproduce perceptions associated with experiences of satisfaction. In a sense, this is merely another way of saying that the primary process works with desiring fantasy: "The first wishing," Freud writes, "seems to have been a hallucinatory cathecting of the memory of satisfaction" (SE, 5:598). The secondary process uses the *detour of thought* to arrive at the satisfaction of desire, and this new mode of desiring requires that the mobility characteristic of unconscious representations be suppressed:

> Thinking must concern itself with the connecting paths between ideas, without being led astray by the *intensities* of those ideas. But it is obvious that condensations of ideas, as well as intermediate and compromise structures, must obstruct the attainment of the identity aimed at. Since they substitute one idea for another, they cause a deviation from the path which would have led on from the first idea. Processes of this kind are therefore scrupulously avoided in secondary thinking. It is easy to see, too, that the unpleasure principle, which in other respects supplies the thought-process with its most important signposts, puts difficulties in its path towards establishing "thought identity." Accordingly, thinking must aim at freeing itself more and more from exclusive regulation by the unpleasure principle and at restricting the development of affect in thought-activity to the minimum required for acting as a signal (SE, 5:602).

Logical connections and substitutive displacements are incompatible with each other. The logical path from one idea to another can be followed only if the intensities of the ideas themselves do not create relations which wreak havoc with the fixed intervals between all ideas. In thought, the instrumental mobility of logic is substituted for the affective mobility of visual representations. To put this in another way: *the secondary process defantasizes desire.* Naturally, we do not mean that there are no fantasies in the conscious mind. However, if one accepts the definition of fantasy elaborated earlier in this study on the basis of Laplanche's suggestive remarks in *Life and Death in Psychoanalysis,* it seems legitimate to think of the secondary process as an attempt to control the agitations of desire, or, more radically, to preserve the self from the disruptive, potentially shattering effects of fantasmatic excitement. And if this excitement is the essence of sexuality, then the development of consciousness may be intrinsically an antisexual phenomenon. Conscious thought does not merely have strategies by which sexual desires are sublimated. The very procedures by which consciousness — and in particular logical thought — establishes relations among its contents depend on a certain neutralization of those contents. What might be called the structuralizing violence of the secondary process desexualizes mental movements.

The temporal implications of the work of the secondary process are accentuated in Freud's later thought. He will come to associate the bound energy of that process with the constitution of the ego; the latter develops by differentiating itself from the id, and it works to inhibit the primary process. Thus we might say that the primary process is not necessarily an unconscious process. It *becomes* unconscious as a result of the operations of the secondary process. We emphasize this point because we wish to argue that *the object of psychic repression is, more significantly than the content of any desiring impulse, the primary process itself.*

The temporal scheme implied here is not without problems: as other writers have noted, it assumes a stage at which an organism would function only on the basis of a total evacuation of all the energy it receives. But it could be argued that the primary process, even before it becomes unconscious, operates not only on the principle of energy totally and immediately discharged, but also on the principle of extremely mobile investments of energy in all the objects and ideas which come to the mind's attention. Freud distinguishes between repression proper and primal repression. The former is the operation by which fantasies or desiring impulses are maintained in the unconscious. The latter — a much more difficult concept to handle — would seem to be an attempted description of how mental activities can become unconscious in the first place. In a 1961 essay on the unconscious ("L'Inconscient"), Jean Laplanche and Serge Leclaire connect primal repression with Freud's notion of a protective shield (*Reizschutz*), the function of which is to preserve the organism from being overwhelmed by external stimuli.[31] It is as if repression first occurred in the service of an efficient economizing of energy. Freud defines primal repression as consisting of "the psychical (ideational) representative of the instinct being denied entrance into the conscious" (SE, 14:148). We wish to supplement this definition by proposing that primal repression takes place when energy is bound, and that the binding of energy is, precisely, a denial of entry into the conscious mind, not merely to specific representations, but perhaps above all to *the multiple relations among representations* which characterize the primary process.

This argument is, we believe, supported by an extremely common phenomenon in Freudian therapy. As patients succeed in making more and more unconscious material available to their consciousness, they discover that they are moving further and further away from the possibility of making a stable formulation of their "problems." At some point, everything begins to mean everything else. Or, perhaps more accurately, each interpretive statement suggests other interpretive statements which are by no means logical consequences of the earlier ones, and which make all interpretation problematic and psychic causation undecidable. There can, for example, be something humorous about the way in which Oedipal feelings jump among various configurations: desire for the father and murderous feelings

118

toward the mother; desire for both parents and, at the same time, murderous feelings toward both parents; identification with the rival *and* with the object of desire; desire to kill the rival and to be killed by the rival; projection into the position of the desired parent who is hurt or even killed by the rival whom the desiring subject has introjected (at the same time that he or she has introjected the hurt, desired parent). The Oedipal triangle is the most stable affective structure uncovered by psychoanalysis, and yet, as everyone familiar with psychotherapy knows, it remains a triangle only in the popular mythology of psychoanalysis. The desiring subject, far from being only one of the three corners of a familial triangle, is always in the process of destroying such a neat configuration and jumping into another corner, or bringing all three corners together into a single, complicated knot, or at the very least switching positions with his or her parental partners in the geometric scheme. Psychoanalytic treatment should *prevent* patients from coming up with their "deepest" desires, for what it should lead them to discover most fundamentally is the impossibility of saying where (and therefore who) the patient is.

In analysis, the inability to locate desire may therefore be the sign of a reactivation of desiring fantasy. Desire is intrinsically a metamorphic activity. Given the profound narrativizing bias of our culture, it is of course not surprising that psychoanalytic treatment has been understood as the unfolding of a psychic detective story: one begins with a problem, works through resistances, and concludes with the saving discovery of a major secret. (The "Freudian" films in vogue during the 1940s — for example, *The Seventh Veil* and *Spellbound* — were constructed along these narrative lines.) The popular view of psychoanalysis represents a cultural repression of the meaning of repression. To a certain extent, however, that view is present in Freud himself. A few pages back we spoke of an uncertainty, in *The Interpretation of Dreams,* regarding the "place" of condensation and displacement in the mind. Freud suggests both that they are primary mental activities and that they are defensive mechanisms by which forbidden thoughts get past censorship and into consciousness.[32] We should now be able to see the extent to which the second view domesticates the first view. For Freud is saying that the primary process enters the dreamer's consciousness only if it is disguised — as the primary process. This tautology is obscured by Freud's distinction between manifest content and latent content. Freud argues that the primary process disguises the dream-thought. But the notion of a perfectly rational dream-thought is a strangely reductive version of Freud's own notion of how the primary process produces meaning. Especially when we remember Freud's insistence that the analysis of a dream will always lead to an unconscious wish, we should find it impossible to separate the dream-thought from the "peculiar" operations which, as Freud himself suggests, actually constitute desires in the unconscious.

It may be true that "the unconscious comprises . . . acts which are merely latent, temporarily unconscious, but which differ in no other respect from conscious ones . . . ," but it is equally true, as Freud writes in the same sentence, that the unconscious also includes "processes such as repressed ones, which if they were to become conscious would be bound to stand out in the crudest contrast to the rest of the conscious processes" (SE, 14:172). It seems to us clear that unconscious *desires* must belong to the latter category. On the basis of both Freud's own definition of desire and the work of recent psychoanalytic theorists (especially in France), we have been elaborating a view of desire as intrinsically mobile, as structurally disruptive psychic displacements. The importance which Freud attributes to "perfectly rational" dream-thoughts in both the formation and the significance of dreams should perhaps be seen as an effort to rationalize the phenomenon of dreaming. To put this in another way, Freud's own speculative procedures enact the very suppressions which he describes. To make the uncovering of logical dream-thoughts the goal of the interpretation of dreams illustrates the immobilization of the primary process. Thus Freud simultaneously asserts the importance of unconscious desire and denies its nature. He narrativizes the primary process by organizing the wildly overdetermined material of a dream around the stable center of a principal desire.

A similar strategy can be detected in the evolution of Freud's view of the process by which free energy becomes bound energy. At first, the unbound energy of unconscious desire is in the service of the pleasure principle; the binding of energy is a response to the requirements of the reality principle. The distinction is convincing. For the manipulation of our environment depends on our failure to respond fully to it, on our being able to fix our attention on relatively stable scenes. But this practical requirement, as Freud appears to recognize, works against the pleasure principle (although ultimately, given the potential destructiveness in the uncontested hegemony of the latter, the reality principle *also serves* the pleasure principle by disciplining it and postponing its operations). In the evolution of Freud's thought, however, the binding process will come to *absorb* the pleasure principle. From 1920 on (with *Beyond the Pleasure Principle*), a new dualism dominates Freud's thought: the dualism of the life instincts (Eros) and the death instincts. The principal object of Eros is to unite, to preserve, to bind; the death instinct breaks connecting links and thereby destroys life. As the word *Eros* suggests clearly enough, sexuality, which had originally been conceived as a disruptive phenomenon, is now on the side not only of the preservation of life, but also of bound energy. Sexuality has become respectable: it is assimilated to the preservation of the human race, and it seeks to establish ever greater unities.

Freud's very appeal, in *Beyond the Pleasure Principle,* to Aristophanes' myth in Plato's *Banquet* is significant. According to that myth, sexual desire is based on an impulse to abolish the difference between the sexes, to reconstitute an androgynous humanity prior to sexual differentiation. The binding process seeks to eliminate difference; it stabilizes and homogenizes. On the other side, free energy has become merely destructive energy. Free energy as the continuously displaced energy of desiring fantasy seems to have been eclipsed by free energy as merely explosive evacuation. It is as if the threat to psychic unity in the mobile energy of the primary process had led Freud to deny the chief characteristics of that process. What we have called the relational frenzy of the primary process has been sublimated into (and canceled out by) the stable unifying structures of Eros.

We are of course not pleading for the "return" of the primary process. Such a plea would be absurd for at least two reasons. First of all, it would have to be based on a historically literal reading of the repression of such activities as displacement and condensation. There can have been no moment in our lives when the primary process was massively repressed, and no period during which it reigned unchallenged in our minds. Our negotiations with the external world undoubtedly require, from the very beginning of life, some binding of the energies of displaced attention. Secondly, and conversely, the primary process is never repressed in the way a specific traumatic scene might be repressed. In the former case, it is obviously not a question of a single representation being expelled from consciousness. Rather, we might imagine a progressive stabilizing of relations among representations. The need to master our environment requires an immobilizing of our desiring responses to our environment. The primary process is thus rejected as a mode of organizing perceptions and memories. But we would argue that it is nonetheless always present in all our responses. For the activities of the primary process are nothing less than the indestructible mode in which human desire is lived. The very functioning of what Freud calls the secondary process depends on a passionate mobility without which there would be no relations to bind in the first place. The secondary process *is* the primary process *mastered*. And the repression of the primary process can never stop taking place, since that repression is the endlessly repeated negation of the way in which our interest in life extravagantly *moves us*. [33]

Art frequently registers that extravagance. The secrets it tells us have less to do with what we desire than with how we desire. But art is of course also composition, and, in the psychoanalytic terms which we have been using, this means that it diagrams processes by which energy is bound. Or, to put this in another way, the work of art could be thought of as an attempt to formalize — to render visible — the masochistic shocks of sexuality. Among the formalizations thus produced are the narrative orders of art. Narrative forms, as we noted earlier, have been associated with realism in art. While the latter by no means exhausts the possibilities of narrative, and while the relation between narrative and realistic effects can be ambiguous and even oppositional, what Gombrich calls the "constant interaction" in the history of Western art "between narrative intent and pictorial realism" is nonetheless a phenomenon worth noting. Psychoanalysis may help us to understand why we find the association between narrative and realism a natural one to make. The narrative structures and sequences elaborated by the secondary process conform to what Freud called the reality principle. They exclude "extraneous" material (or relegate such material to backgrounds); they teach us how to center objects on which we wish to focus our attention; and they provide a formal model for the carrying out, in time, of our projects toward the world. Such techniques of exclusion, of centering, and of a linear progression toward goals are the preconditions for our manipulative recognitions of and negotiations with reality, although this is by no means identical to saying that they adequately diagram either our perception of the world or our passionate interest in it.

Assyrian sculpture has allowed us to see that the movements mastered by the secondary process persist in the very orders which deny them. We naturally do not mean that the perceptual displacements which we have been tracing can be identified with the specific contents of particular desires. Rather, we have wished to suggest that the mobile attention required by the palace reliefs replicates, within the formal terms of esthetic vision, the psychic moves which characterize the fantasmatic excitements of desire. In subverting the narrative priorities of an art in which narrative centers are almost always spectacles of violence, the spectator's visual mobility forestalls a mimetic fascination with those spectacles, a deeply sympathetic intuition of the pleasure in destruction. The impressive achievement of the Assyrian sculptors is to have given an apparently unquestioned importance to narrative organizations at the same time that they guide us away from the scenes of violence which they meticulously and deceptively center. In so doing, Assyrian art suggests the exact way in which the activities described by Freud as belonging to the primary process can function not in the unconscious or in dreams (or in jokes or slips of the tongue), but rather *within* the rational organizations of the secondary process. The mobility of desire means that we are always moving away from the presumed objects of our desire; fantasmatic excitement is a continuous snapping away from the sources of that excitement, a potentially endless series of productively mistaken replications.

In nonpsychoanalytic terms, one might speak of something at once simple and radical, and immediately verifiable in the most ordinary human consciousness: a certain indifference to the objects of our attention, a readiness to continue substituting one image for another. A kind of restless attention is perhaps a sublimated version of desire's mobility, a desexualized, purely formal imitation of sexual self-displacements and self-shatterings. Thus, if we follow the cues in Assyrian sculpture which encourage the spectator's visual mobility, it is perhaps because we are less concerned with stable designs and narrative certainties than we have been encouraged to believe. We swerve away from scenes of violence as we do from all other scenes. And this continuously mobile attention disrupts those orders which hypostatize violence as climactic events or epitomes in human experience.

This mobile attention, which we have traced in our readings of various scenes from Assyrian sculpture, could also be accounted for within a general theory of perception. Julian Hochberg, arguing against "the Gestaltist's model of the nervous system, in which object properties are explained in terms of simultaneous interactions that occur within some hypothesized field within the brain," points out that objects are "examined by a succession of multiple glimpses." Hochberg maintains that ". . . the integration of the successive glimpses that we receive when scanning a picture must depend on our ability to fit each view into some 'mental map,' into a cognitive structure that stores the information that each glance brings," and that explains the *"highly skilled sequential purposive behaviors"* in visual perception.[34] This view has obvious similarities to Gombrich's notion of "scanning," of proceeding from random readings of pictures to the search for a coherent whole. Finally, Gombrich himself is indebted to James J. Gibson, whose work on perception led him to conclude that, in seeing, we proceed from the vague and the general to the articulate and the differentiated. In *The Perception of the Visual World,* Gibson writes that ordinary perception is characterized by frequent zigzags and irregular jumps; the sequence of our visual fixations seems to be more or less random. What we learn to do is to produce a differentiated and structured scene from these random sequences.[35]

From the point of view adopted in our discussion of Assyrian sculpture, it could be said that the principles of narrative powerfully aid this structuring process; they reorient our zigzags and irregular jumps into meaningful scenes. In a sense, the antinarrative mobility which we have found in the palace reliefs works against the way in which we have learned to see; it reestablishes, within a defined esthetic space, some of the perceptual habits which Gibson associates with the visual world rather than with a visual field (we get the latter, he writes, when we fixate a point and take note of the experience). The Assyrian palace reliefs thus provide a particular case of what we take to be a general esthetic paradox: the "mobile syntheses" of art (to adopt a term from Mallarmé) return us, in part, to a "preesthetic" vision. Or, more accurately, they lead us to conclude that the esthetic includes a certain eruption of the errant, and the erratic, within an *already* framed and composed field.[36] Theorists of perception speak of a progression from random sequences to structured scenes. Art, we would argue, problematizes this structuring movement toward what Gombrich calls a "coherent whole." Like all great works of art, the Assyrian palace reliefs simultaneously display and render unfathomable the formative or ordering powers of art. They draw our attention to a certain repudiation of form in art, to an enigmatic equivalence between formal elaborations and a continuous slippage of significance away from any locatable forms. The visible, material artifacts of esthetic history are, in a nearly inconceivable way, a repository of invisible and immaterial experience: an experience of form and sense not as the end (the goal and the conclusion) of a process, but rather as the continuously disappearing intervals of permanently restless perception and thought. Finally, an argument could be made for criticism as a type of reflective analysis which locates the erasures of form in art; and, to return once more to a psychoanalytic perspective, we might say that criticism makes manifest the ontology of human desire by tracking down the threats to its visibility in art.

124

The Restlessness of Desire

We have, however, been educated to feel uneasy about our perceptual and affective mobility. We are expected to isolate and to study what is most serious and most important in our lives, to bind the "irresponsibly" diversified paths of our interest into structures of high human significance. But, in denying our natural tendency to swerve, what might be called the narrative morality of our culture tends both to atrophy our sense of reality and to increase the risk of our mimetic fascination with scenes of violence. In this study, our concern has been primarily with representations of violence in art and, more generally, with cultural discourses *about* violence. We naturally do not claim to be offering a blueprint for dealing with physical violence; furthermore, when we speak of swerving away from scenes of violence, we are not proposing an indifference to real historical violence. Of course, we believe that the way we represent and speak about violence is not unconnected to historical outbreaks of violence, although it would be absurd to argue that a certain type of representation leads directly to violent or nonviolent behavior. Ultimately, however, the effects of our attempts to diminish violence in history may depend on our fundamental imagination of violence: on how we define it, on whether or not we allow ourselves to be fixated by it, on how we see its relation to other kinds of experience. And there is no reason to believe that a reeducation in the *moves* of a consciousness less constrained by the orders of narrativity would have chaotic or explosive effects. For in a sense the very restlessness of desire is a guarantee of its curiously mild and pacific nature. Intrinsically, desire is perhaps a form of violence — of psychic disruptiveness or self-shattering — *without a place,* and which therefore never succeeds in taking place. The fantasies of desire are always mistaken replications of its objects, and these mistakes could be thought of as an ontological safeguard against a fanatically organized interest in any part of the world. Such beneficent errors are perhaps crucial to the surprisingly austere sensuality of art: a sensuality which gratifies our appetites by moving us away from the objects which might have satisfied them, and which thrives on the somewhat abstract nourishment of intervallic memories and anticipations.

"Betweenness"
in the Palace Reliefs

As a final example from Assyrian sculpture, consider the striking representation of a lion being released from a cage in Figure 52. (For a discussion of the relation between this scene and the scene just below it on the palace wall, see page 57.) There is a powerful narrative line here: both the man and the lion direct our attention toward anticipated scenes of action to the left. The cages function as immobilizing frames, and in a sense the narrative movement in this scene is antiesthetic. It is as if violent pressures inherent in the action being represented made representation itself impossible; we have two picture frames in the process of being abandoned by their subjects.

And yet we are also drawn back into the frame — without, however, being forced to substitute a pictorial immobility for narrative movement. First of all, in terms of mere quantity of space, the nearly abandoned cages occupy almost the entire scene. Partly because of the prominence given to the repeated lines and forms of the two cages, they can compete for our attention with the dramatic subject in which they play only an accessory role. Above all, the lion's progress is strangely arrested by a certain confusion between his body and the bars of his cage (see Figure 53). An undisturbed narrative reading would require a clear sense of the lion *behind* the bars of his cage. In fact, his resemblance to the cage is emphasized by the blurred distinction in the relief between foreground and background. The next to the top bar in particular seems to be an extension of the lion's body. At the same time, however, the leonine aspect of that bar is qualified by its relation, simply as a curved line, to the straight line across the top of the cage. We have, as it were, an overdetermined curve: it is simultaneously a nonfigurative line, the bar of a cage, and part of an animal's body.

The inside of the cage is thus transformed from a narrative space (bars in the foreground, moving lion in the background) into a continuous esthetic space of related forms. We are kept within the frame, but its contents have, so to speak, become extremely active without contributing to narra-

126

tive movement. This activity is purely relational. It consists of contacts among juxtaposed forms, contacts which suggest a certain irrelevance in the anecdotal distinction between the animate and the inanimate. The lion, it might be said, leaves his cage by remaining within it, by the peculiar way in which he almost becomes his cage. As we have frequently seen, relations make identities somewhat uncertain. Or, more exactly, the subject of the scene *is* its denarrativization; that is, the process by which we substitute a reading of related fragments for the reading of a coherently structured anecdote.

Nonetheless, the narrative power of Figure 52 remains very strong. The movement toward the outside of the cage may very well strike us as more dramatically delineated than the relational activity we have just mentioned. Not only is the subject of the lion leaving his cage emphasized by the human figure's repetition of this action; we might also note that all the horizontal elements help to guide our attention to the long horizontal shape of the emerging animal's body. Furthermore, formal relations by no means only denarrativize the scene. The virtual diagonals which connect the lion's face to the man's face and the lion's front paw to the top left of the man's cage have the effect of intensifying our attention to the most dramatically narrative aspects of the scene (that is, to the man — or child — opening the cage and the lion leaving it). There is in fact a complex diagonal structure in Figure 52. We have not only the lines just mentioned, but, as the design in Figure 54 indicates, one might also trace diagonals in the opposite direction, from the lower right to the upper left. The elements of this second diagonal structure focus our attention on spaces devoid of or relatively weak in narrative interest (we are thinking of the space between the upper right corners of both cages, as well as of the insides of the two cages where, as we suggested a moment ago, the dramatic subject is subordinated to a play of repeated lines and related forms). Finally, many of the diagonals we have traced either meet in or pass through, or close to, the near-rectangle to the left of the man's cage, and this small empty space thereby becomes a focused element in the scene.

Figures 52 and 53: King Ashurbanipal fighting lions on foot and pouring a libation over dead lions. (Description of a three-register composition. Ashurbanipal shoots an arrow at the lion emerging from the cage in the left section of the upper register. Details of Figure 29.) *From the North Palace of Ashurbanipal at Nineveh.*

Figure 52

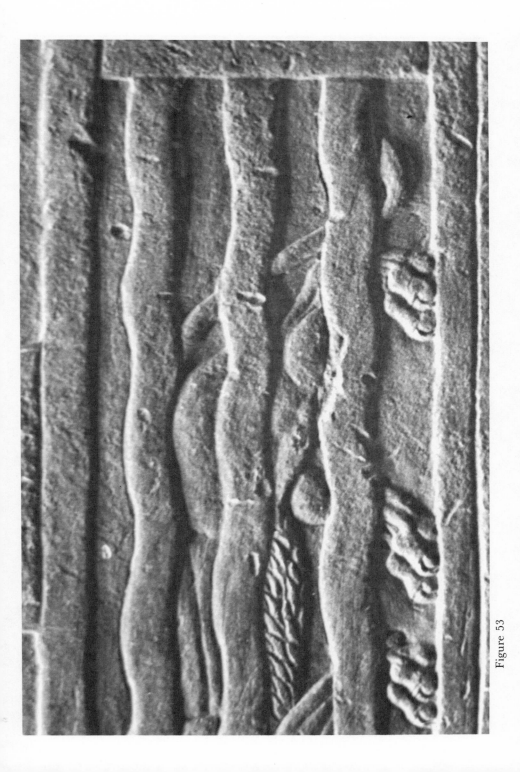

Figure 53

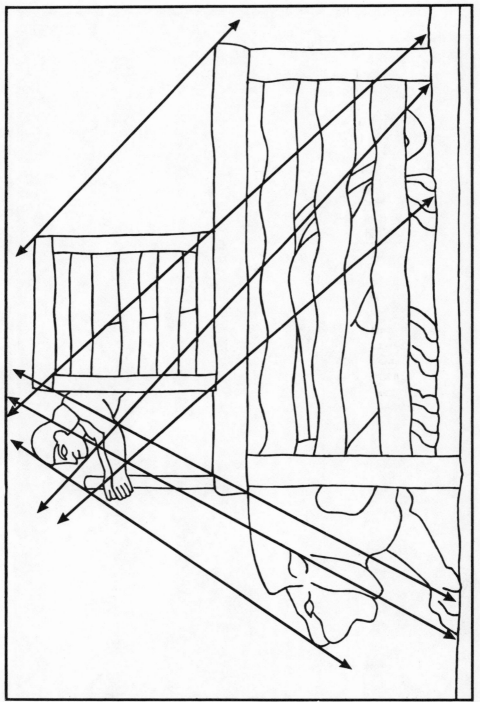

Figure 54

In conclusion, we might consider the emphasized emptiness of that space as emblematic. The near-rectangle is a cage which imprisons nothing. It is an insignificant focal point designed to scatter rather than to concentrate our attention. It is an ambiguously centered space surrounded and even constituted by strong narrative elements (its upper border represents the scene's principal action: the opening of the lion's cage), at the same time that it is "crossed" by virtual diagonals which redirect us to the predominantly formal relations and the floating identities of the two cages. We might say that the interpretive location of that actively empty form is somewhere between two very different readings of the scene. It is a space which mediates between two modes of attention: a narrative vision which organizes forms into the elements of a story, and a more agitated, erratic vision which substitutes related and continuously shifting bits and pieces for the wholeness of being and linear movement of narrative forms.

We have emphasized the second mode, for, in our culture, it is more neglected than the first; most importantly, it has provided us with the perceptual model of an alternative to a fascinated, mimetic relation to violence. We may, however, end with a more conciliatory remark, and note that the peculiar impression of balance and sanity which the Assyrian sculptors give us may be due to their willingness not only to fracture their subjects but also to feast us with images of a perhaps inherently thrilling narrative violence. The nearly indefinable quality of "betweenness" in the palace reliefs may, then, manifest an impressive hesitation or even ignorance, on the part of these anonymous ancient artists, about the forms of disruption and of violence which they have chosen to love.

Figure 54: Diagonal structures of Figure 52.

131

Notes

1 R. C. Barnett, *Assyrian Palace Reliefs and Their Influence on the Sculpture of Babylonia and Persia,* translated by Christina Haglund (London, 1960), pp. 13–14.

2 H. W. F. Saggs, *The Greatness That Was Babylon: A Sketch of the Ancient Civilization of the Tigris-Euphrates Valley* (New York, 1967), p. 95.

3 Eva Strommengen, *Five Thousand Years of the Art of Mesopotamia* (New York, 1964), p. 42.

4 André Parrot, *Nineveh and Babylon,* in *The Arts of Mankind,* edited by André Malraux and Georges Salles, translated by Stuart Gilbert and James Emmons (London, 1961), pp. 12–13.

5 Strommengen, *Five Thousand Years of the Art of Mesopotamia,* pp. 10–11.

6 A. Leo Oppenheim, *Ancient Mesopotamia: Portrait of a Dead Civilization* (Chicago, 1964), p. 232.

7 André Malraux, Preface to André Parrot, *Sumer: The Dawn of Art,* in *The Arts of Mankind,* p. xxvii. As a final note to this obviously incomplete review of critical commentary on the art we will be examining, we might refer the reader to Hans G. Güterbock's contribution to a Symposium on Narration in Ancient Art, "Narration in Anatolian, Syrian and Assyrian Art," *The American Journal of Archeology,* 61, no. 1 (January 1957): 62–71. Also, Anton Moortgat has a few pages on the style of the palace reliefs (more specifically, on what he refers to as their "rhythm") in *The Art of Ancient Mesopotamia: The Classical Art of the Near East,* translated by Judith Filson (New York, 1969); see in particular pp. 134–37. A short chapter on the rendering of spatial relations in Assyrian art can be found in H. A. Groenewegan-Frankfort, *Arrest and Movement: An Essay on Space and Time in the Representational Art of the Ancient Near East* (Chicago, 1951). Finally, our discussions of the Assyrians' treatment of narrative subjects obviously neglect the decorative schemes of the palaces and the religious reliefs. In his study of *Reliefs From the Palace of Ashurnasirpal II* (Archiv für Orientforschung, Beiheft 15 [Graz, 1961]), John B. Stearns argues against the "unfortunate misunderstandings" to which "preference for the freedom of expression of the narrative reliefs as opposed to the formalism of the religious reliefs" has led. Having posited the cruelty of war and the hunt as the principal theme of the palace reliefs, historians have gone on to conclude that . . . "such irrelevant cruelty explains the collapse of the Assyrian empire" (p. 60). As we shall see, the argument against such naïve ideas of "prevalent cruelty" in art and their presumed historical consequences can be made on the basis of an analysis of the very reliefs—those depicting war and hunting—which have given rise to these ideas.

8 Speaking of the way in which the royal marksman and his attendants infallibly spear and fling arrows at enraged lions, R. D. Barnett asks, in *Assyrian Palace Reliefs in the British Museum*

(London, 1970), pp. 31–32: ". . . what are we to make of this, on the whole, slightly improbable scene of wholesale slaughter by a royal huntsman of unerring skill, dressed in such unsuitable attire? Is it simply a sort of ritual or symbolic scene, . . . in which the king is traditionally pictured as defender of his people and their flocks against the beasts of the untamed desert? Did it really happen? Or was it merely the exaggeration and flattery suitably offered to an Oriental despot? No doubt it is best to regard it as intended magically to ensure that what ought to happen, does." Barnett returns to the question again in his indispensable work on the *Sculptures From the North Palace of Ashurbanipal at Nineveh (668–627 B.C.)* (London, 1976), pp. 12–13. The ideological function of the violent stories told in Assyrian sculpture from Ashurnasirpal to Ashurbanipal has been persuasively argued by Arlene D. Wynter. The historical representation of Assyrian narrative art "became carriers of the prevailing ideology on a public scale" ("Royal Rhetoric and the Development of Historical Narrative in Neo-Assyrian Reliefs," *Studies in Visual Communication,* 7, no. 2 [Spring 1981]: 31.

9   "Instincts and Their Vicissitudes," *The Standard Edition of the Complete Psychological Works of Sigmund Freud,* 24 vols., edited by James Strachey (New York, 1976), 14:129. Page references to *The Standard Edition* (henceforth abbreviated as SE) will be given in the text.

10   Jean Laplanche, *Vie et mort en psychanalyse* (Paris, 1970), p. 155. Translated by Jeffrey Mehlman as *Life and Death in Psychoanalysis* (Baltimore, 1976).

11   Freud does, however, occasionally refer to a *qualitative* peculiarity in sexual pleasure. The question is discussed — in an irresolute, even tortuous manner — in the *Three Essays on the Theory of Sexuality* (1905); and in "The Economic Problem of Masochism" (1924) Freud speculates that the "qualitative" aspect of pleasure may lie in "the rhythm, the temporal sequence of the changes, rises and falls in the quantity of stimulus" (SE, 19:160).

12   Laplanche, *Vie et mort en psychanalyse,* pp. 164–65.

13   In "Dostoevsky and Parricide" (1928 [1927]), Freud speaks of Dostoevski's "boundless" sympathy for the criminal as "identification on the basis of . . . murderous impulses similar to those of the criminal — in fact, a slightly displaced narcissism. . . . This may," Freud adds, "be quite generally the mechanism of kindly sympathy with other people . . ." (SE, 21:190).

14   Marquis de Sade, *The 120 Days of Sodom and Other Writings,* translated by Austryn Wainhouse and Richard Seaver (New York, 1966), p. 200.

15   E. H. Gombrich, *Art and Illusion: A Study in the Psychology of Pictorial Representation,* Bollingen Series 35, no. 5 (Princeton, N. J., 1960), pp. 129, 131, and 136.

16   See Roland Barthes, "L'Effet de réel," *Communications* 2 (1968), and Michael Fried, *Absorption and Theatricality: Painting and Beholder in the Age of Diderot* (Berkeley and Los Angeles, 1980), p. 194, n. 88; "Painter into Painting: On Courbet's *After Dinner at Ornans* and *Stonebreakers,*" *Critical Inquiry* 8, no. 4 (1982): 619–49.

17   Frank Kermode has impressively argued for the power of such conventions in our culture in *The Sense of an Ending* (New York, 1967). Are narratives ever neutral? See Hayden White's compelling argument in an issue of *Critical Inquiry* devoted to narrative (7, no. 1 [1980]: 5–27) for the intimate relation between narrativity and the impulse to moralize reality.

18   Among the numerous studies of narrative codes and narrative transformations in contemporary criticism, we might mention Tzvetan Todorov, *The Poetics of Prose,* translated by Richard Howard (Oxford, 1977). Some of Todorov's essays in this collection treat the complications of narrative which we have just mentioned.

19   The peculiarly casual way in which Alain Resnais re-presents filmed documents of Nazi atrocities in his 1955 film *Nuit et brouillard* could be taken as another example of this perspective, in art, on historical violence. By his filmic understatement of an especially brutal version of such violence, Resnais actually prevents us from taking a safe distance from Nazi atrocities — a distance which a melodramatic highlighting or emphatic centering of that violence might have facilitated.

20   Marcel Proust, *Remembrance of Things Past,* translated by C. K. Scott Moncrieff and (for *Le Temps retrouvé*) Frederick A. Blossom, 2 vols. (New York, 1924), 1:628–29. *À la recherche du temps perdu,* edited by Pierre Clarac and André Ferré, 3 vols. (Paris, 1954), 3:835–36.

21   *Ibid.,* 2:1008–9; and 3:889.

22   Riefenstahl has always claimed to be a nonpolitical artist. "I am not a political girl," she stated in a 1965 interview for *Film Comment;* "I am not interested in the politics" (3, no. 1 [Winter 1965]:8). In the same issue, Ulrich Gregor objects strenuously to the view of Riefenstahl as "a misunderstood genius and martyr" and attacks "the obstinate estheticizing attitude" of film historians who ignore "the political and ideological context" of Riefenstahl's films (pp. 24–25). A few pages later, Robert Gardner does not even bother to "estheticize" Riefenstahl's work in order to defend her: he finds her "gentle," if "childish," and even suggests (seriously, as far as we can make out) that "if she believed the Nazi myth it was because she thought it was a better road to health and physical fitness" (p. 30). In an interview with Michel Delahaye for the September 1965 issue of *Cahiers du cinéma,* Riefenstahl emphasized once again that *Triumph of the Will* is "history. A purely historical film" (170:49). Our point has of course been that it is not a question of choosing to emphasize either the "esthetic" side of Riefenstahl's work *or* its "political context"; rather, her political sympathies are perfectly clear from a purely esthetic analysis of her films.

23   For an elaboration of this argument about realistic fiction, see the chapter "Realism and the Fear of Desire" in Leo Bersani, *A Future For Astyanax: Character and Desire in Literature* (Boston, 1976).

24   In the case of railroad tracks extending away from us toward the horizon, we have the impression of parallel lines coming together and finally meeting. The apparent diminishing of the space between the two tracks could be thought of as promoting a narrative effect: we are perceptually locked into a certain space which we follow until it is erased by the "climactic meeting" of two parallel lines.

25   For an interesting and often quoted discussion of the history and function of the frame, or, more exactly, of the "variants of the frame-field relation in art," see Meyer Schapiro, "On Some Problems in the Semiotics of Visual Art: Field and Vehicle in Image-Signs," *Semiotica* 1, no. 3 (1969): 223–44.

26   In a very different esthetic context, this notion is developed in Leo Bersani, *The Death of Stéphane Mallarmé* (Cambridge, 1982).

27 Sandor Ferenczi spoke of this double direction during intercourse as a tension between "urethral" and "sphincteric" phenomena: "Everything points to the fact that the urethral (i.e., ejaculatory) tendency is at work from the beginning, throughout the entire frictional process, and that in consequence an unceasing struggle occurs between the evacuatory and the inhibitory purpose, between expulsion and retention, in which the urethral element is eventually victorious. This two-fold innervation might, among other things, manifest itself also in the to-and-fro motion of the frictional process, in which penetration would correspond to the ejaculatory tendency, withdrawal to an ever recurring inhibition" (*Thalassa: A Theory of Genitality,* translated by Henry Alden Bunker [New York: 1968], p. 8).

28 Many readers are undoubtedly familiar with Ernst Kris's notion of controlled or regulated regression, in which the ego, instead of being overwhelmed by the primary process, creatively uses it (see his *Psychoanalytic Explorations in Art* [New York, 1952]). Anton Ehrenzweig goes further than Kris in arguing for "the eminently constructive role of the primary process in art"; for Ehrenzweig, "what is missing in Kris's concept . . . is the insight that creativity does not merely control the regression towards the primary process, but also the work of the primary process itself " (*The Hidden Order of Art: A Study in the Psychology of Artistic Imagination* [Berkeley and Los Angeles, 1967], pp. 31 and 261–62). Finally, Jean-François Lyotard has made an extremely stimulating argument for what he calls the *double renversement* (the "double reversal") of unconscious processes in art. To the extent that art merely repeats the contents of unconscious desires, it can be read symptomatically. More interesting for Lyotard (and for us) is *the nonrealization of desire in art.* By repeating the movements of desire rather than its hallucinatory contents, the work of art prevents desire from settling into any constituted, definitive meanings; it is as if unconscious desire were emptied of its specific representations by becoming the object of its own characteristic mode of operation (see Jean-François Lyotard, *Discours, figure* [Paris, 1971], and "Oedipe juif" in *Dérive à partir de Marx et Freud* [Paris, 1973]).

29 We realize the problems involved in speaking of an "uninterpreted" description of a dream. The most unanalyzed account of a dream is already different from the dream "as it took place." It is probable (although inherently unprovable) that no account is ever given of the latter, and for therapeutic purposes this is no loss, since the patient's "distortions," associations, and interpretations are at least as important for analysis as the hypothetical "dream-in-itself." For an early phenomenological critique of Freud's distinction between manifest and latent content, see Georges Politzer, *Critique des fondements de la psychologie* (Paris, 1928).

30 There is, however, some hesitation in Freud about where to locate the censoring function. In the development of Freudian theory, it would seem to prefigure the superego (and Freud explicitly recognized the connection), but, in *An Outline of Psychoanalysis* (1940), for example, the censoring function in dreams is spoken of as originating in the ego.

31 Jean Laplanche and Serge Leclaire, "L'Inconscient," *Les Temps modernes* 17, no. 183 (July 1961): 81–129.

32 We have found that an argument similar to ours is made by Merton M. Gill, although he does not conclude, as we do, that what he calls the "apparent contradiction" in Freud's views of the primary process (a contradiction which he seeks to resolve) amounts to an attempted taming or domestication of unconscious processes. See "The Primary Process," in *Motives and Thoughts: Psychoanalytic Essays in Honor of David Rapaport,* edited by Robert R. Holt, *Psychological Issues* 5, nos. 2-3, Monograph 18/19 (New York, 1967).

33   Other writers have questioned the notion of an absolute ontological difference between primary and secondary processes. Robert R. Holt, arguing against a view of the primary process as "chaos, random error," even speaks of its "systematic character." See "The Development of the Primary Process: A Structural View," in *Motives and Thoughts*. Max Schor, in *The Id and the Regulatory Principles of Mental Functioning*, in *Journal of the American Psychoanalytic Association*, Monograph Series, no. 4 (New York, 1966), develops a similar view of the id (as an organization rather than random chaos); the id can of course be considered as the successor to unconscious primary processes in Freud's later structural view of the mind.

34   Julian Hochberg, "The Representation of Things and People," in E. H. Gombrich, Julian Hochberg, and Max Black, *Art, Perception, and Reality*, edited by Maurice Mandelbaum (Baltimore, 1972), pp. 60, 63, and 68.

35   James J. Gibson, *The Perception of the Visual World* (Boston, 1950).

36   In a recent review of E. H. Gombrich, *The Image and the Eye*, and Rudolf Arnheim, *The Power of the Center*, Rosalind Krauss refers to "a skepticism that a whole generation of younger art-historians now feels with regard to the usefulness of an analysis of representation by means of an appeal to the ahistoricism of a psychology of vision. . . . The visuality of the visual arts is an historical, cultural, not a natural, construction. And the deconstruction of this institution is a vastly different enterprise from the analysis of visual perception, which assumes its relevance to the subject by insisting that art is visual perception completed" ("Seeing as Believing," *Raritan* 2, no. 2 [Fall 1982]: 84–85). David Summers has pushed this "deconstructive" activity to the point of arguing for "the possible semantic structure of planarity itself," and against a view of the picture plane as the "natural" vehicle for illusionistic space (see "The 'Visual Arts' and the Problem of Art Historical Description," *Art Journal* 42, no. 4. [Winter 1982]: 9–10.) What we wish to suggest here are some of the ways in which art *undoes* its own constitutive semantic structures. Our brief reference to a psychology of perception is not meant to suggest an indifference to the ways in which the "visuality" of the visual arts is, as it were, historically constructed, but rather to refer to a movement of retreat within the work of art from the very terms of intelligibility which constitute it — a move toward the undifferentiated and unconstituted, toward a perhaps mythically "preesthetic" perceptual (or linguistic) wandering.